THE
FORECLOSURE
DEFENSE GUIDEBOOK

An EASY to Understand Guide to
Saving Your Home From Foreclosure.

Written in Layman's Language

Vince Khan
Consumer Defense Programs

ISBN: 145647006X

ISBN-13: 9781456470067

Library of Congress Control Number: 2011901271

Consumer Defense Programs is a homeowner advocacy group helping homeowners fight bank fraud. For more information about Consumer Defense Programs,
visit: www.ConsumerDefensePrograms.com

WHAT OTHERS HAVE SAID ABOUT THIS BOOK

Wow! This is amazing—and outrageous! It was very easy to read and understand.

Thank you Vince for bringing this truth out. And for your humanitarian and courageous stand to keep people from losing their homes to corrupt predator lenders!

Cindy W (online comment)

Thank you for the serious amount of work put into this book. I seriously believe that this type of information provided free to the people is one of the hallmarks of truth. Another hallmark of truth is simplicity. I'm sure you know from experience the convoluted path you had to follow to unwind the web of deceit woven by the banks to conceal this fraud being perpetrated since the repeal of Glass/Steagall. The book is simple, easy to read, and easy to understand.

Mark (online comment)

Absolutely phenomenal reading! I have passed this info on to everyone that I can think of! This is the kind of educational material that has the ability to really change things in this country and beyond!

James - Mississippi

I got the book last Tuesday and I went through it twice...lots of information and well put together. Thank you for all of the hard and time consuming work you have put into educating homeowners. ... Thanks again for the great information you have provided. Take care and may God bless you always.

Patricia Y - California

WOW.... I'm blown away with the content. THANKS ...for showing me the way.

James - Colorado

We are very happy to have a guid book to have as a reference to this subject. It is very tricky. We have been fighting for our home and cannot believe how the average person does not know this stuff!

May God bless you and your team for what you are doing to help others. We have forwarded this book to everyone we know and have asked them to pass it along to their friends and family... It is important information that everyone needs to know...

Once again, thank you from the bottom of our hearts!

Jeff K

Thank you for the book. It was very well written and easy to understand. I am a legal researcher and paralegal and although I am comfortable with reading statutes and case law, I realize many are not. This book also clearly lays out the point by point bread trail that the banks have done with the note through the securitization process. WOW!!!

Frank (online comment)

Opened it, read it, and am absolutely blown away!

Tom (online comment)

I couldn't stop reading. What a wonderful resource that is an easy read & easy for everyone to understand. This book is so timely and helpful to all of us in a tough spot these days. The book really broke things down in layman terms. Thanks again for providing this for us.

Bridget (online comment)

This possibly the best gift ever. I can only "THANK YOU" for the truth, and the direction, that I must take on MY house. May The Father In Heaven continue to help you.

Andy (online comment)

Disclaimer ← IMPORTANT

HELP, I AM FACING FORECLOSURE.

Knock, knock came the noise from the front door. I gingerly opened the door to find my postman handing me an envelope requiring my signature. It was for certified mail.

It was a Notice of Default from my servicer. It felt as if someone had physically punched me in the gut and I felt like vomiting. Intellectually, I knew this moment would arrive, but yet I cannot help the way I feel.

I couldn't even get myself to finish reading the rest of the document before tossing it on my desk and crawled into bed and cried.

As a grown man, I cannot recall when the last time I cried. I've been conditioned to "be a man" and not to break under pressure. But, despite it all, I cried. Somehow, I wish that someone would come and tell me everything is going to be OK, just like my mother did when I was a little boy. Unfortunately, no body could. Because nobody understands what I am going through. It's hard to "keep it together" when your whole world is falling apart around you.

My name is Vince Khan. This is my story.

I made a lot of money around 2002-2004. I made enough money to retire for the rest of my life. With that money, I invested in a number of properties, partly as a way to park my money and partly as a way to make a little money investing in real estate.

In 2009 I started another business that required a lot of start up capital. Things didn't turn out as I had planned. I had invested all my money into the venture but it was not enough. I needed more money. In 2010, I made a decision to stop paying the mortgage for 4 of my investment properties to feed my new start up, in the hopes that eventually, my startup would turn around and I would then have enough money to pay back the bank.

I was wrong. My startup failed. **Not only had I lost everything**, I was heavily in debt because I leveraged everything I had to fund my company.

So, like millions of people around the country, I was facing foreclosure.

Shortly after I stopped making payments, I started looking at my options. I could either do a short sale (meaning I could sell the property for what is owed) or just hold onto the properties for as long as possible before they foreclose on me. Or I could put up a fight.

I chose to fight.

To be honest, when I started this journey, I was just as ignorant as everyone else who was in going through a default. I borrowed the money. Now, for one reason or another, I can't pay my mortgage. So, I was lead to believe that the bank was entitled to foreclose on my houses and repossess them.

I was wrong.

It was at that time that I started learning about bank fraud. At first, **I was skeptical but I kept an open mind**. As I dug deeper into this issue, it became clear that there was more than meets the eye. I started reading more and more instances of homeowners winning in court against banks. In fact, I discovered that banks have sold mortgages onto Wall Street as what's called "mortgage backed securities" (MBS). At first, I did not know what that meant. My thoughts were, "so what?"

As I studied this issue deeper, I came to realize that banks were actually committing some very clever schemes to steal people's home without the proper "Standing" to do so.

You see, once a bank have sold a promissory note as a MBS, it no longer owns the note. And if it does not own the note, it does not have the right (or Standing) to foreclose.

But they do this every single day, because **they rely on our ignorance**. They rely on **your ignorance**. They rely on the judge's ignorance and they even rely on their own lawyer's ignorance to pull this scheme off.

On one side, we have a growing population of people living in tent cities without running water, without toilets or other things you and I take for granted.

At the other end of the spectrum, we have bank executives getting multi-million dollar bonuses for how quickly they can foreclose people's homes (without having any actual legal authority to do so).

Not only that, these bank executives have received TRILLIONS of taxpayer money from TARP (the Troubled Asset Relief Program) to pretty much do as they see fit. You know, buy up smaller banks, buy executive jets, go to the Bahamas for exotic retreats and other wonderful ways to spend the handouts from our government.

This got me mad.

But most frustrating of all, I discovered that as a homeowner, my choices were very limited.

Firstly, even if I took the time to learn about this fraud, so what? How does this have to do with me saving my houses from foreclosure? I am not a lawyer. I am too poor to afford one, and even if I had $25,000 to retain one, there was no assurance of success. (Access to the law is no longer affordable to the common man).

Secondly, I don't know enough about the law to put up a viable defense. I'm just your average computer geek. I don't know anything about the law. I don't have the time or the mental energy to learn to be a lawyer to put up a defense.

Thirdly, there was very limited information available for homeowners to learn about this stuff. Even if one has the time, it would take a full time occupation to figure all this stuff out at the best of times (ie. When one is not suffering from crippling depression when one's world is falling apart).

Fourthly, very few attorneys even know about this stuff. There wasn't really anyone I could go to to learn this information.

The odds were just stacked against me.

Faced with insurmountable adversity, I was faced with a decision: To give up or to go down fighting.

My father told me a story about how Japan won so many battles in Asia (they took over almost all of Asia before America dropped the bombs). He said that unlike other armies, the Japanese doctrine was "death before dishonor". The concept of surrender or retreat was the lowest of shame for a Japanese soldier. When they landed their troops into a battle, the Japanese would tell their soldiers that the only way they would go home was to either win, or return in a body bag. <u>There was no retreat</u>. As a result, the Japanese soldiers fought like their lives depended on it, because it literally was.

For me, this was the doctrine in which I lived my life. I either succeed in what I do or I die trying. As Master Yoda said in "The Empire Strikes Back", "do or do not, there is a try."

So, study I did.

I committed to doing whatever it takes to put up a fight and win.

I started to challenge the bank using the processes outlined in this book, and to cut a long story short, I managed to compel the bank to issue a Rescission of the Notice of Default on my property.

Essentially, this means that the bank can not foreclose on my house and it is currently in limbo.

As of the time of writing, I am in the process of filing a civil action called a "Quiet Title Action" to remove the lien on the house. You can read more about the progress of this on my website at www.consumerdefenseprograms.com.

As I learned more about this subject, it occurred to me that millions of other people around the

Division of Chief Deputy Clerk
Lane County Deeds and Records

$67.00

RPR-RESC Cnt=1 Stn=9 CASHIER 06
$10.00 $20.00 $10.00 $11.00 $16.00

RESCISSION OF NOTICE OF DEFAULT

Reference is made to that certain Trust Deed in which ████████ █████ , ██████ ████ was grantor, WESTERN TITLE & ESCROW COMPANY was Trustee and MORTGAGE ELECTRONIC REGISTRATION SYSTEMS, INC. was beneficiary, said Trust Deed recorded on ██████████ or as fee/file/instrument/microfilm/section No. 20██-██████ of the mortgage of records of Lane County, Oregon and conveyed to the said Trustee the following real property situated in said county:

LOT ██ █████ SK█████ ██ FIRST ADDITION, AS PLATTED AND RECORDED IN BOOK ██, PAGE 4, LANE COUNTY OREGON PLAT RECORDS, IN LANE COUNTY, OREGON.

Commonly Known As: ██████ ██ ████ ██
EUGENE, OR 97███ ████

A notice of grantor's default under said Trust Deed, containing the beneficiary's or Trustee's election to sell all or part of the above described real property to satisfy grantor's secured by said Trust Deed was recorded on ██████2040, in said mortgage records or as fee/file/instrument/microfilm No. 20██-██████: thereafter by reason of the default being cured as permitted by the provision of Section 86.753, Oregon Revised Statutes, the default described in said notice of default has been removed, paid, and overcome so that said Trust Deed should be reinstated.

Now therefore, notice is hereby given that the undersigned Trustee does hereby rescind, cancel, and withdraw said notice of default and election to sell; said Trust Deed and all obligations secured thereby hereby are reinstated and shall be and remain in force and effect the same as if no acceleration had occurred and as if said notice of default had not been given; it being understood, however, that this rescission shall not be construed as waiving or affecting any breach or default (past, present or future) under said Trust Deed or as impairing any right or remedy thereunder, or as modifying or altering in any respect of the terms, covenants, conditions or obligations thereof, but is and shall be deemed to be only an election without prejudice, not to cause a sale to be made pursuant to said notice so recorded.

IN WITNESS WHEREOF, the undersigned Trustee has hereunto set his hand and seal: if the undersigned is a corporation, it has caused its corporate name to be signed and its corporate seal to be affixed hereunto by its officers duly authorized thereunto by order of its Board of Directors.

world were going through the same problems I was going through. The biggest issue faced by distressed homeowners was that there was no easy to understand, easy to follow materials available to the average homeowner to put up a fight against lender fraud.

With this in mind, I put together a blog online to help homeowners. All the sudden, my site got bombarded with so many people wanting to know more about what I've discovered. Everyone started to ask me questions; everyone wanted me to help them with their situation.

I quickly realized there were a number of problems with this situation.

1) I barely have enough headspace to deal with my own problems, let alone other people's.

2) If I answered people's questions openly, the BAR Association would love to put a stop to this by accusing me of "practicing law". (Competition is bad for business after all.)

3) Helping people takes time, and everyone's situation was different. I only have a limited amount of time in the day. I barely had time to pee, let alone help other people.

4) Helping people for free full time means I cannot spend that time to make a living for myself. It is a full time job just to keep up with all the research and reading to understand the strategies of foreclosure defense.

With these problems in mind, I decided to write this book. My goal is to give homeowners an **easy**

to understand resource so that they can quickly grasp how the fraud is being perpetrated. Once they understand the fraud, to then teach them how to articulate a viable defense. I've written this book so that anyone can put together a viable strategy to defend their home from lender fraud and so they can keep their home for as long as possible.

Unlike other books, this book is written in a conversational tone using lots of stories and analogies so everyone can understand. I believe that often "less is more" when it comes to information. While other books are hundreds of pages long, this book by comparison is rather small. Too much information leads to overwhelm and "paralysis by analysis". My goal is to make this handbook be a **practical guide with real practical steps you can do right now** to save your home, yet be **easy enough to digest in one evening's reading**.

Please keep in mind, this whole scheme was created by the brightest minds in the banking industry. This is something banks don't want the public to know. They have gone to great lengths to make sure people like you don't know about their schemes. Court cases have been settled with conditions of a gag order are being done on a regular basis. In one instance, an expert witness I've interviewed have had his life threatened by banksters for the information he knows.

The information presented in this book is highly controversial. *I truly believe that I am writing this book at great risk to my own personal safety*. Thanks to the power of the Internet, my hope is that once this book is in the hands of enough people, that the banks will not feel the need to "silence me".

I've always been inspired by the story of Jesus. In particular, his bravery for doing what's right in the face of overwhelming adversity. Jesus was arrested for talking against the rabbis and was condemned to death. His jailer knew that Jesus was a good man and did not want to see him dead. The jailer deliberately left Jesus' jail door open and made arrangements for Jesus to easily escape. Instead of running away, Jesus stayed in his cell and ended up dying on the Cross.

This is true bravery.

While I don't want to be a martyr, I do feel strongly about helping homeowners despite the dangers to myself.

If you are facing foreclosure and want an easy to read, and easy to understand guide to help you stay in your home, then this book is for you. Too often, one has to wade through thousands and thousands of pages of information to get a basic understanding of what's going on. This type of information is often written in legalese (by lawyers for lawyers) and is ladened with double talk jargon that it is hard for the average person to comprehend.

I hope you will join me in standing up against injustice and bank corruption. And if this book makes a difference in your life, please "pay it forward". Please tell others about it.

Vince Khan

TABLE OF CONTENTS

CHAPTER 1:
UNDERSTANDING THE
SECURITIZATION PROCESS

You are facing foreclosure. You don't have a lot of money or a lot of time and you can't afford to hire a lawyer. And even if you could afford one, it is very hard to find a lawyer who knows enough about bank fraud to help you.

This is where we begin our journey. Before we delve into the nuts and bolts about your options, we first need to understand how the fraud is being committed. Once we expose the fraud, then you will know how to articulate a viable defense. That's why we start this chapter by diving into the securitization process and what it means. It is fundamental to exposing the fraud.

To fully comprehend the arcane wizardry and myth that encompasses the securitization process in relation to the right to enforce a negotiable instrument (a promissory note), this chapter is designed to support the legal argument behind *who is the real and beneficial party of interest.*

BACKGROUND AND INTRODUCTION

In 1933, the Glass-Steagall Act was enacted to regulate the FDIC and banking. Specifically, it governed the protection of depositors' monies so that banks were not allowed to gamble with the money in their safekeeping. This means banks could not trade their assets on Wall Street.

In 1999, the Glass-Steagall Act was repealed and another bill was introduced; known as Gramm–Leach–Bliley Act. This effectively allowed banks to package and *securitize* their loans onto Wall Street.

This means that suddenly the trillions of dollars from Wall Street could be used to fund loans. (*This is a good thing.*) This means that more loans were available to more people.

This means that Retirement Funds, Hedge Funds, and all sorts of institutional investors had a "safe" place to park their money...these safe places would come to be known as mortgage backed securities (MBS). (*This is also a good thing.*)

These institutions demanded banks make these mortgage backed securities packages available to them. These institutions relied on the following:

1.   The bank's banking license
2.   The bank's underwriting process
3.   The bank's collections infrastructure

(*This is a good thing.*)

Things started to break down when banks realized that since they were not required to be left holding the bag at the end of the day, they could simply underwrite any old loan from any idiot who can sign their name to paper. Banks decided to change their underwriting guidelines around 2001-2002 (Bush era). (*This is where things started to go downhill.*)

You can read more about this at this link as Allstate Insurance is now suing Countrywide. http://www.forbes.com/2010/12/29/allstate-sues-bank-of-america-over-countrywide-losses-marketnewsvideo.htm

This means any McDonald's burger flipper could go down to the bank and get a loan for $1,000,000 with "no money down." (*No offense to those working in the fast food industry.*) These were commonly known as *liar loans* in the mortgage industries. This is great for low income earners as long as the housing market is in a boom growth curve. This gets really bad in a housing bubble where the price of housing is way beyond the affordability index of most households' median income.

INCENTIVE AND MOTIVATION OF SECURITIZATION

When a bank lends you money, they traditionally get 2.5 times the face value of the loan over 30 years. Not bad, considering that they did not use a single red cent of their own money. It is all digitally created through the Federal Reserve System (read *Modern Money Mechanics* published by the Federal Reserve).

For example, if you borrowed $100,000... over 30 yrs, you will have paid around $350,000 to the bank. Look at the Truth in Lending disclosure statement from your loan documents.

Because of the Gramm–Leach–Bliley Act, banks are now able to sell mortgage backed securities. Some bright people at Goldman-Sachs and others in the financial industry came to the conclusion that they could make even more money if they could sell loans on Wall Street, and so they did.

This book is the story of what happened.

Instead of making 2.5 times over 30 years from money they did not put up, banks decided they could **make up to 1.5 times the face value of the loan immediately**. Just package these loans and sell them on Wall Street. As the market grew, they not only made money from the sale...but also from the appreciation of the stock (they are allowed to hold up to 10% of the security to qualify as a sale under Financial Accounting Standards).

THE GAME OF GREED

Under the Fractional Reserve System, a bank can lend up to 9 times the face value of their depositors' money or cash reserves.

Instead of receiving 2.5 times over 30 years for a loan, banks suddenly realized that they could make even more money if they sold the loan and received the CASH NOW.

Fractional Reserve Banking Explained

Under the guidelines of the Federal Reserve, a bank can lend up to 9 times the amount of their depositors' money. In other words, if you deposit $1 into your bank...they can lend up to $9 out. Currently, in the US, the reserve ratio is 10:1 or 10%.

So, from that $100,000 loan, they receive $150,000 cash. This is treated as a deposit, which means they can now lend out $1.35 million (9 times $150,000). And do it again, and again. Lather, rinse and repeat. (*This is really good for the bank. This is really good for borrowers as there is a sudden glut of unlimited money to borrow from. This is really bad for the economy in the long run, as we will see.*)

If you study basic Economics 101 in high school, you will know that if you have too much money chasing limited goods, it leads to an increase in prices. Well, this is exactly what happened.

The banks threw their underwriting guidelines out the window. They had what's called a *fiduciary responsibility* to ensure that the loans were properly underwritten. This means that they were supposed to make sure loans they underwrote were backed by people who could actually afford to pay it back. Instead, they just ignored these underwriting guidelines in the name of greed.

The banks knew that these loans were destined for Wall Street, and that they were not going to keep the loans...so it suddenly became a game of hot potato, as "it became someone else's problem."

They basically stuck it to Wall Street.

This means they stuck it to your retirement fund, your stock portfolio and your life insurance portfolio.

It was the perfect set up for the biggest financial meltdown in the history of mankind. **It was the perfect storm.**

Before we go into the financial meltdown of 2008-2009, let's talk about the Securitization process and how it relates to your loan and bank fraud.

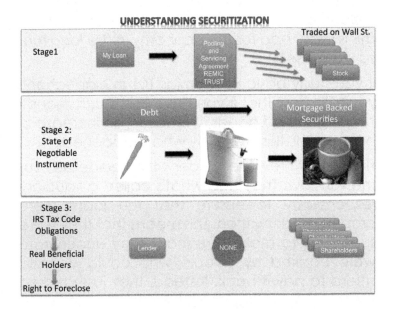

UNDERSTANDING SECURITIZATION

STAGE 1: THE POOLING AND SERVICING AGREEMENT PROCESS

Once a loan is closed, it quickly gets put into a Pooling and Servicing Agreement. This is then registered on the SEC as a REMIC Trust. REMIC stands for *Real Estate Mortgage Investment Conduit*. It is known as a Special Purpose Vehicle for the purpose of tax exemption purposes. I will explain why this is important in Stage 3.

They appoint a master servicer of the REMIC and a Trustee to manage the Trust. Normally, the Trustee of the Trust has the power and responsibility to administer the assets of the Trust.

For example, back in the Feudal Lord days, these Lords would create Trusts to put their assets (such as their land, their castle, and so on) into. In the event something happened to the Lord, the Trustee had the power to manage the estate/trust.

However, in the case of a REMIC, the Trustee **does not have the power to manage the assets of the Trust**. We will discuss in Stage 3 how this is different.

Once this REMIC is formed, it then gets converted into a security that is traded on Wall Street. This will make more sense later when I explain the relationship between an investor, a shareholder and a REMIC.

STAGE 2: THE CHANGING OF THE STATE OF THE NEGOTIABLE INSTRUMENT

Imagine if you will, that your loan is a carrot. It gets thrown in with thousands of other carrots into a giant juicing machine called a REMIC. At the end of the process, you get gallons and gallons of carrot juice. This juice is then sold to hundreds of people.

This is what happens to your loan when it gets securitized. Your loan is now owned by thousands of shareholders all over the world.

Furthermore, the state of the loan is changed. **Your loan has been converted into a stock.**

This is **REALLY REALLY important**. Please spend a moment to understand this. Re-read this section several times if you need to.

Your loan is no more. It is now and forever a stock.

In other words, <u>you cannot make a carrot from carrot juice</u>. What's done can never be undone. (Unless they somehow were to buy back all the stocks outstanding for the REMIC).

Once a loan has been securitized, it forever loses its security (i.e., the Deed of Trust, or the ability for the bank to foreclose on your house). This will be explained in Stage 3.

According to the Milken Institute, using data from the Federal Reserve, over 85% of subprime loans have been securitized. This is why I say that <u>over 85% of foreclosures are done fraudulently</u>.

A loan is what's called a *negotiable instrument*. There are specific laws governing negotiable instruments called the Uniform Commercial Code. Specifically, the right for a bank to enforce and foreclose on a property is subject to the claimant being a *real party of interest.* For the party to be a creditor of a negotiable instrument, there needs to be a proper chain of endorsement from the original lender to the party wishing to enforce the note.

If the loan has been sold, then the bank can no longer claim that they are a real party of interest.

Not only that, once a loan has been converted into a stock, it is no longer a loan. If both the loan and the stock exist at the same time, that is known as double dipping. Double dipping is a form of securities fraud.

A negotiable instrument can only be in one of two states when it undergoes securitization, **not both at the same time.** It can either be a loan (and treated and governed as such) or a stock (and treated and governed as such). Once it is traded as a stock, it is forever a stock. It is treated as a stock and regulated by the SEC as a stock.

On your Deed of Trust or Mortgage, it has language that says something like "This Deed of Trust secures a Promissory Note."

Listen, when that promissory note got converted into a stock…that promissory note no longer exists.

If a Trust was created to secure a promissory note, and that promissory note is destroyed…then that Trust is invalid. The Trust secures nothing.

The Deed of Trust is what your lender uses to give them the right to foreclose on your house. If the Deed of Trust is invalid, then the lender loses their right to foreclose on your home.

STAGE 3: REAL PARTIES OF INTEREST

Let's talk about accounting rules, specifically the rule governing a sale. To prevent accounting fraud, various governing bodies created Financial Accounting Standards (FAS). As you know, accounting is a very important area that needs to be regulated tightly to prevent companies from cooking the books.

Specifically, FAS 140 was created to govern the sale and securitization of a negotiable instrument. Look it up. Google FAS 140.

One of the things about FAS 140 is the rule governing a sale. A transaction can only be recognized as a sale if it is sold to a party at arm's length. In other words, you cannot sell an asset to yourself (this is what Enron did to hide their losses). Also, it says, (and I am paraphrasing) that once an asset is sold, the seller forever loses the ability to control the asset.

To illustrate this point, imagine if I were to sell you a brand new laptop. You took the laptop, and smashed it to a million bits with a sledgehammer. Because I sold the laptop to you, <u>I have no say whatsoever about what you do with the laptop. It is yours.</u>

This is really important to understand.

Once an asset has been sold, the <u>seller forever loses control of the asset</u>.

What that means is, if your lender sold your loan to a REMIC, then they forever lose their ability to enforce, control or otherwise foreclose on your property. Put simply, they are no longer the real party of interest. They are just a servicer.

So Who Are the Real and Beneficial Parties of Interest?

Before we can properly answer this question, we have to discuss IRS tax codes.

You see, the real party of interest has to pay taxes on their earnings.

In other words, if your bank owns your note, they have to pay tax on the interest earned from that note. If a REMIC owns your note, then the REMIC has a tax liability.

To avoid the problem of double taxation, banks put these loans into SPVs (special purpose vehicles) so they don't get taxed on them. This is covered under Internal Revenue Code 860.

This way, <u>only the shareholders are taxed</u>.

This means, **only the shareholders are the real parties of interest.**

In the previous section, I discussed the powers of the Trustee. Because of this special IRS rule, the Trustee is not the real and beneficial party of interest because the REMIC does not own the notes, the shareholders do; therefore they cannot enforce the promissory note.

The Case of Double Taxation

Corporations have known for years about double taxation. This means, at a corporate level, at the end of the year they take all the revenue, and subtract the expenses; what's left are the profits. These profits are then taxed.

The corporation also has shareholders. The corporation typically distributes dividends to their shareholders. Once the shareholders receive their dividends, this is considered to be income to the shareholders. This is also taxed.

In other words, profits are taxed twice.

In other words, they can't have their cake and eat it too. They can either accept double taxation and let the REMIC hold the centralized power, or they can distribute the tax liabilities to the shareholders, in which case they have also distributed the parties of interest.

The bank chose to have a distributed party of interest scheme to avoid paying taxes twice. (*There is nothing wrong with this.*)

But now they have a real pickle. If no one entity is a real and beneficial party of interest, then each and every shareholder of the REMIC is.

So then the question is...who has the right to foreclose?

The answer is...**no one.**

If the thousands of shareholders each own a tiny part of your promissory loan, can any one of them foreclose on your house? No.

A promissory note is only enforceable in its whole entirety.

That is the nature of the fraud being perpetrated before the American public and worldwide.

REMIC, INVESTORS AND SHAREHOLDERS EXPLAINED

There is a lot of confusion around the concept of securities conversion, specifically around the various parties involved, such as the investor and the shareholder.

This chapter explains in greater detail how each of these entities tie in together.

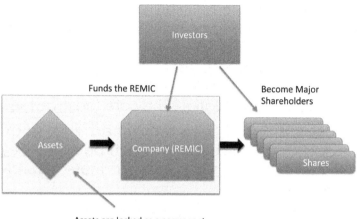

Funds the REMIC

Become Major
Shareholders

Assets are locked as a permanent
attachment to the REMIC

To illustrate the point, let's use another analogy. Let's say I am Steve Jobs in the 1970's. I come to you asking for $1000 to invest in my little company called Apple. Part of Apple's assets is the intellectual property and design of the Apple computer.

10 years later, we go public. Because you were my initial investor, your initial shares are now worth a lot of money. We then convert your percentage of ownership as an investor into publicly tradable stock.

Imagine, however, if immediately after I go public, I create another company and assign the intellectual property and design of the Apple computer to this new company. Is that legal?

The answer is no. That's commonly known as *bait and switch*. You cannot register one thing with the SEC and market the stock...and then after the money is transferred, switch out the asset.

How this relates to a REMIC is this: there are two pseudo government entities called Fannie Mae and Freddie Mac (these are actually privately owned companies). These two giants fund or invest in most of the REMICs created for the purpose of securitization. They are the <u>investors</u>.

Once the REMIC gets converted into stock, Freddie and Fannie get very rich because <u>they are the majority shareholders</u> of these publicly traded stocks.

When a REMIC is formed, its assets (your loan plus thousands of other people's loans) are declared a permanent fixture to the REMIC. (*This is like that intellectual property of Apple computer.*) This is registered with the SEC. It is public information. In other words, once an asset is registered and traded as part of the security, you can't just switch it out because it has become a permanent fixture of the traded asset.

The conclusion I want you to take away here is that an asset declared in an SEC filing is permanently attached. **This is a permanent conversion**. This means there is no doubt that your loan/promissory note is no more.

Let's take a case of double existence to illustrate the point. Let's say we have the stock traded on Wall Street (that supposedly contains the note). Next, we take the promissory note and we assign it to another bank, who takes it and securitizes it again.

If this situation were to happen, the same loan would be traded *twice* on Wall Street. In other words, the second set of investors got duped. They bought a lemon. They basically bought a forgery.

This is securities fraud. It cannot happen.

THE REPURCHASE AGREEMENT

Let's talk about the Repurchase agreement clause in the Pooling and Service Agreement that created the REMIC.

There are typically clauses within the Pooling and Service Agreement governing both the submission into as well as the repurchase mortgages. Let's spend a few moments analyzing these because it is very important that you understand these terms in your foreclosure defense strategies (and if need be, articulate your defense).

When your original lender (called an Originator) sells your loan into a REMIC, they are required to:

1) Deliver your promissory to the REMIC within 90 days. This means that the Originator has to endorse the promissory note using the language "pay to the order of" to a **NAMED PARTY**.

2) They have to physically deliver your note to the REMIC.

3) State law requires that they also record this delivery in your County Recorder's office.

In 99% of the time, all three things were never done. This leads to a defect in the chain of title.

Next, let's talk about the repurchase of the promissory note out of the REMIC.

There **are no clause in any Pooling and Servicing Agreement that I have been able to find that**

governs the event of default that gives the servicer the right to repurchase the note in default. This is because this event is governed by FAS 140. In other words, the "lender"/servicer cannot just repurchase your loan out of the REMIC. Remember, the sale has to be done to an arms length third party. And if you sell something, you can't take it back. The only time you can take it back is if it was defective.

So let's look again about what a typical Pooling and Servicing Agreement says about defective repurchasing of mortgages. If an instrument is found to be defective (meaning it did not fulfill the above 3 required steps), the originator is required to buy the note back at <u>full face value</u>.

Let's use an analogy to illustrate this point. If I sold you a computer for $1000 and you take it home, turn it on, and nothing happens...then it can be proven that I sold you a defective product and you are entitled to your $1000 back.

If after 4 years (assuming I gave you a 5 year parts warranty), the computer refuse to boot, you can still come back to me (because of the defect) and ask for your money back (or I can replace the part). As you know, in the computer industry, a 4 year old computer is very out of date and is worth only a fraction of the original price...but I still have to give you your money back at full $1000 purchase price.

But, if through no fault of my own, your computer broke, then I am not bound to honor the warranty. For example, if you dropped the computer and it broke, then that's just tough luck on you.

If you then list your broken computer on craigslist for $20, and I see it, then there is nothing stopping me from buying it back. But I would never buy it at the original $1000 price, that's just silly.

In other words, a loan that is in default is never worth as much as a good performing loan. It has to be bought back in its defective status.

Using this analogy, we can see that if a loan was to go bad (default) through no fault of the Originator, there is no clause that requires the Originator to buy back the loan.

We can also see that the Originator/servicer does not have to buy back the note at the same price it sold into the REMIC. It is buying the note back as a nonperforming asset at best at a substantial discount.

WRITING OFF A BAD DEBT

Next, let's talk about how I can make the claim that the shareholders and/or the REMIC wrote off the nonperforming debt to receive a tax credit. There is no specific evidence or law that backs up this argument; just something I call "condition precedent".

For years, physicists have postulated that there were these things called "black holes" but no one was able to find one. You see, a black hole is a collapsed star that is so dense that no light can escape it. And because we depend on light to see, no one could actually "see" a black hole until one day, somebody discovered this phenomenon called the "event horizon". It is the line in which the gravitational pull of the black hole equals the strength of the light trying to escape from the black hole. Because of the existence of the event horizon, people then concluded that there **must** be a black hole inside the event horizon.

Using this condition precedent, I will illustrate why it is in the interest of the REMIC to write off a debt rather than to try to collect it in a foreclosure.

Let's say you are a farming supply shop owner and I come to you asking for credit. We've known each other for years, so you say, "sure". I used your credit to buy some seeds and fertilizers for my farm. Sadly, we had a flash freeze this year and all my crops died. So, I owe you $100 but I cannot pay you and go out of business. As a business owner, you can do one of two things.

1) Carry the debt as an asset.
2) Assign it to a third party through endorsement
3) Write it off as a loss, and then sell it off to a debt collector

That's it. So let's look at each of these cases.

If you carry the debt as an asset...then you do not get tax credits for the loss. My purchase of seeds still counts as revenue for the purposes of taxes. Ie. You are taxed on money you did not received.

If you assign it to a third party endorsement, then I will owe the money to the third party. The requirement is that I signed a promissory note, and you physically endorse the note to the other party. In this instance, the debt between you and I are settled. I now owe the third party. You cannot write off the loss as a tax write-off.

If you write the debt off as a loss, then you not only do you <u>not count my purchase as revenue</u>, but the loss you suffered through the bad debt is offsetted against other income.

As we discussed earlier, the REMIC can not foreclose because the real parties of interest are the shareholders. So, in order for them to realize any benefit from a nonperforming note is to sell it to another party in full so that that party may be able to collect (foreclose) on the debt.

The REMIC can either sell it as a perfect debt or a written off debt. <u>A perfect debt is one that the REMIC and the shareholders do not receive any tax credit</u>. When the REMIC sells the perfect but nonperforming debt, it will only receive pennies on the dollar as our previous example with the faulty computer.

Or, the REMIC <u>can sell the debt as a written off debt, receive tax credit for the sale, AND receive money from the buyer of the nonperforming note</u> for pennies on the dollar.

If it were you, what would you do? Either way, you are receiving pennies on the dollar, ie. about the same amount. Might as well get the tax credit for it, right?

That is why I believe that the shareholders and the REMIC are actually writing the debt off, and then selling it onto the servicer who attempts to foreclose on the property as if it was perfect. It's not.

BUT CAN THEY FORECLOSE?

Let's take a skeptical look at our analysis.

Let's say that the individual shareholders **did not write the asset off** and indeed did sell the non-performing note back to the bank wishing to foreclose on your home.

Does this give them the right to foreclose on your home?

The answer is still no.

EVEN IF the bank is able to resolve the following issues:

1) The original delivery of the title of the promissory note has to be properly done within 90 days of sale into the REMIC. If this was not done, this meant that the chain of title was broken, leading to a defective instrument. Therefore, they cannot foreclose based on a defective instrument.

2) The bank has to prove that the loan was not written off by the REMIC. This is very difficult to do.

3) The bank has to prove there is a perfected chain of title from origination, to the REMIC, and from the REMIC back to the bank. You and I know that this is never done properly.

They still have this problem of CFR Title 12: Section 226 (included in the Appendix).

> § 226.39 Mortgage transfer disclosures.
>
> (a) Scope. The disclosure requirements of this section apply to any covered person

except as otherwise provided in this section. For purposes of this section:

(1) A "covered person" means any person, as defined in §226.2(a)(22), that becomes the owner of an existing mortgage loan by acquiring legal title to the debt obligation, whether through a purchase, assignment, or other transfer, and who <u>acquires more than one mortgage loan in any twelve-month period</u>. **For purposes of this section, a servicer of a mortgage loan shall not be treated as the owner of the obligation if the servicer holds title to the loan or it is assigned to the servicer solely for the administrative convenience of the servicer in servicing the obligation.**

More than likely, your servicer buys back notes on a regular basis. Ie. More than 1 mortgage in any 12 month period.

If the servicer buys back a loan for administrative purpose ie. To foreclose, then they do not have the rights of the owner of the obligation. ie. They do not have the right to foreclose.

So, as a foreclosure defense, it is up to you to challenge the bank to prove all of these points.

If on your Notice of Default or Substitution of Trustee, the documents mention someone like New York Bank Mellon Trust Series 123223, then this will indicate that the servicer is foreclosing on behalf of a REMIC. And as we know, the REMIC can not foreclose because it owns "carrot juice" (ie. The shareholders are the true party of interest).

If you are in a judicial State and when you confront the bank regarding Standing, and they say "we bought the note back so we can foreclose", then challenge them to prove that the loan has not been offsetted as a bad debt through both a Request for Admissions and Request for Production of Documents asking for accounting records of the chain of action within the REMIC. We have this process outlined in our automated coaching program within the membership program on www.consumerdefenseprograms. com.

If the bank gives you some answer like "the investor for this loan is Fannie Mae", they are bringing fraud before the court. As we discussed earlier, the investor is not a real party of interest.

CONCLUSION

So let's summarize our points. Since over 85% of loans have been securitized, we now know that banks are not the real parties of interest in any foreclosure transactions. Neither are the investors of the REMIC. No one can foreclose.

When a loan goes into default, the REMIC writes it off. Once an asset is written off, the shareholders receive tax credits from the IRS. This means that the note is settled. The Note is gone.

The only way a bank can foreclose on you is if they buy the promissory note back from REMIC as a written off debt, just like a debt collector would. Tax credit has been given to the shareholders and the REMIC. It is no more. So, essentially, these banks are picking up the promissory note for pennies on the dollar and through deceit, they try to reattach the converted loan to the dead Trust/Mortgage. They then take these documents and represent them to the world as if they are the real parties of interest. They bring these documents into court, deceiving the court and their own counsel (who, for the most part, is ignorant of this scheme).

Look, the servicer/"pretender lender" would not willingly disclose any of this stuff to you or to the court during a foreclosure.

1) They never tell you who the holder in due course is. At best, they tell you who the investor is. As we know, the investor is not the holder in due course and does not have the authority to enforce the note.

2) They do not disclose whether they own the note or acting as a servicer to enforce the note. Often times, they are just acting as a servicer with no authority to enforce the note. Remember, if the note is held by the REMIC, it is unenforceable.

3) If they bought the note back for the purpose of foreclosure in truth (and not as an administrative procedure), then they never disclose whether the debt was written off by the REMIC...or whether the proper chain of title can be demonstrated.

This is how banks steal your house, and the houses of millions of families around the country.

This means, if you are facing foreclosure, you need to learn the truth about your loan and learn how to fight for your rights.

This means that if you have lost your home due to foreclosure, you might be a victim of fraud and be entitled to punitive damages of up to 3 times the value of your loan.

So, let's summarize to see how this all works together. The bank originates the loan and sells it to the REMIC for 1.05 to 1.5 times the face value of the loan. It got paid in full (and more). Then, when the loan goes into default, it picks up the note pennies on the dollar, forecloses on your house, and then sells it to the next sucker for full price. Oh, did I mention that FDIC covers between 70% to 80% of the loan amount also?

Wow. You got to tip your hat to them. From a purely technical business stand point, that's just utter brilliance.

This is why I want to share this information with you so you know you've been conned.

You have a right to be angry. You SHOULD BE!

CHAPTER 2: THE BUBBLE BURST OF 2008-2009

No one was complaining when things were going strong. Everyone was happy. Everyone had a home. Housing prices were growing in double digits. Until...the house of cards came tumbling down.

No one can pin it to a specific date, but sometime in 2008, things started going downhill. The bubble had gotten to a point where more and more homeowners were realizing they can no longer afford multi-million dollar (artificially inflated) homes on a minimum wage income. More and more homes were beginning to go into default.

As more and more loans went into default, this affected the value of the mortgage backed securities (MBS). You see, the shareholders and investors of these stocks made **three fatal assumptions** about what they bought:

1) They assumed that the bank did the right thing in their underwriting process. They didn't.

2) They assumed that once a loan in their portfolio went into default, they were able to foreclose and cover their losses. They were wrong.

3) They assumed that this ride would never end. It did.

Once Wall Street investors realized they could not cover their losses (by foreclosing on their underlying assets), they became very upset (and rightly so). They started suing the banks and stopped buying these toxic assets.

Investors stopped buying these MBS. Soon, the pool of money dried up. Soon, no one could get loans, not even those with 800 plus FICO scores.

Then house prices started to plummet...

THE 3 TRILLION DOLLAR BAILOUT (TARP)

As more investors sued these banks, things got ugly. This is the Day of Reckoning for our banker friends. It's time to pay the Piper.

The banks got scared. All their greedy scams had finally caught up with them.

So, they got together and bribed Congress to bail them out, threatening that if Congress didn't, we would have a financial Armageddon; the Fall of Wall Street. Everybody's retirement funds would immediately be wiped out. Put simply, "they were too big to fail."

Donald Trump said it best. "When I borrowed $100,000 and I defaulted, it was MY PROBLEM. When I borrowed $100 million and I defaulted, it became THEIR PROBLEM."

Faced with a no win situation, Congress quickly signed the TARP (Troubled Asset Relief Program) bailout which authorized the Federal Reserve to give over $900 billion to the banks in the first round. We now know that the Federal Reserve Bank has since given over $3.5 TRILLION dollars to the banks with very few strings attached.

Congress (and the American people) were lead to believe that once the TARP money got to the banks, they would start lending money again. They didn't.

The banks were given "free money" from the Taxpayers to pretty much "do with as they see fit." They could give bonuses to top executives. Go to the Bahamas for a retreat. Buy jets. Buy up smaller banks. Invest in gold. They were able to do whatever they wanted with the money with no strings attached.

As housing prices kept dropping, many low-income homeowners (as well as real estate investors) got caught. No one expected the bubble to happen. Everyone thought this ride would never end. Low income homeowners and investors alike would buy any property at almost any price, knowing that they could sell the property a few months later for more than what they bought the property for in a hot market.

Now, homeowners and investors find themselves with properties that are worth significantly less than what is owed.

Worse, many homebuyers and investors went into the game with negative cashflow business plans. Their expected exit strategy was through price appreciation in an appreciating market.

When the capital markets dried up, no one could get loans. Since housing prices are dependent on people's ability to secure loans, when people could no longer get loans, no one could afford to buy houses.

Thus we find ourselves in a housing crisis today. The markets that experienced the highest growths, specifically California, Nevada, Florida and Arizona are also the ones with the highest foreclosure problems.

Currently, millions of families are faced with an unrealistic burden for mortgage payments well beyond their income ratio. Added to this, millions of families are out of work due to the contraction in the economy as the market is correcting itself into a true equilibrium.

As more and more families find themselves in financial trouble, the rate of real bank defaults is much higher than what the banking industry would like us to believe. Many people are months, if not years behind on their payments but banks are not ready to foreclose and declare these loans delinquent.

As more and more loans go into default, more and more homeowners are fighting back. More people are learning about loan fraud and securitization, but until now, few people could fully comprehend the mechanics of how the fraud was being perpetrated.

This is the reason why this book is being given to you and why people are passing this book to everyone they know. I am exposing the fraud for the first time in simple English so people can understand.

CHAPTER 3:
BANK FRAUD EXPOSED

So, now that I've explained the securitization process, you are probably more informed about this problem than most judges and attorneys. You see, most people just don't know about this scam that is being perpetrated on the American public. I hope that you use this opportunity to get informed. Tell your friends about it. Talk about it to your neighbors. Write to your Congressperson. Next time you are at a social gathering, bring this up. This is the only way we wake up America.

So let's summarize in case you missed it:

When a loan has been securitized, it got converted from a debt into a stock. The real and beneficial parties of interest are the individual shareholders holding a fraction of the note. Therefore, no one person may foreclose on the property.

But wait a minute. If this is the case, why are there so many houses being foreclosed on every day? Even today, despite the robo-signer scandals?

The problem goes way deeper than robo-signers. Not only are loan assignments not properly assigned and recorded, they do not even have the right to do so.

Remember FAS 140? Once an asset has been sold, you forever lose control over that asset. If it is sold into a REMIC, how can the bank (who is no longer the real party of interest) foreclose?

They can't.

They get away with it every single day because they rely on our collective ignorance.

They rely on your ignorance.

The judge's ignorance.

The attorney's ignorance.

The foreclosure and mortgage industry personnel's ignorance.

It's time to wake everyone up.

GIVE ME A FREE IPOD

Let's talk about the difference between an investor, a shareholder and a real party of interest.

When your loan is underwritten, the bank needs investors to initially provide the money to fund the transaction. Oftentimes this is Fannie Mae and Freddie Mac. They put up the initial cash so that the REMIC can buy these loans. This security is then traded on Wall Street. In other words, when the REMIC got converted into a stock, the investors make money because they got in on the ground floor investment. Buy low, sell high. In many cases, they became the majority shareholders of these REMIC Trusts.

So, let's talk about the rights of a shareholder by using Apple stocks as an example. Let's say you own 1000 Apple shares...and Apple advertises that they historically pay about $1000 per month in dividends.

Let's say after a couple of months, Apple had a bad quarter and stops paying you your $1000. And the next month, it doesn't get better. They now "owe" you $2000.

Does this then give you the right to go into an Apple store and pick up a new Mac laptop and an iPod?

The answer is...you'll likely get arrested for theft.

This is the same thing with shareholders of a REMIC.

A shareholder of an asset cannot just go to the store and pick up goods as recompense. This means the individual shareholders cannot dip in and touch the loan/asset. Besides, they own "carrot juice," remember? This means they own a little bit of thousands of loans.

So, let's look at the cast and crew of the heist. We have the following characters:

- The Lender
- The Investor
- The Shareholder
- The REMIC
- The Trustee of the REMIC
- The Servicer

The Original Lender Can Not Foreclose

As I discussed earlier under FAS 140, the original lender sold it to the REMIC and forever lost their rights to enforce the note.

The Investor and Shareholder Can Not Foreclose

As I illustrated with the Apple and iPod example, while the investors and shareholders as a whole are the real parties of interest, individually they cannot just come in and foreclose because they only own a tiny portion of your loan.

The REMIC and the Trustee

Remember, the REMIC holds all the loans together in a pooling and servicing agreement. However, because they chose to avoid the IRS tax rules (I.R.C 860) for double taxing, they pass on the real party of interest/ownership of the asset to the individual shareholders. So neither the REMIC nor the Trustee may foreclose.

The Servicer is Not a Real Party of Interest

The Servicer can only collect the money and pass it to the REMIC. That's the extent of their job.

So, Who Can Foreclose?

The answer is: <u>nobody</u>.

Oftentimes you will hear the bank respond to enquiries as to who the real party of interest is by saying, "Fannie Mae is the investor." They are technically not lying. This is true. But, as I illustrated earlier, an investor becomes a majority shareholder of the traded stock...but they are not a) the holder in due course or b) the real party of interest.

This is the lie that banks are bringing before the court every single day.

Only the true and beneficial holder in due course is the real party of interest. Not the investor.

Again, if the bank is not the real party of interest, nor the holder in due course...what business do they have foreclosing on your house?

If Fannie Mae and Freddie Mac are not the true and beneficial holder in due course, how can foreclosures be done in their name?

This is the **scam bankers don't want you to know**.

THE GREAT PRETENDER LENDER SWITCH

This is how the scam is perpetrated by your so-called lender. They advertise that they offer loans. They work with the mortgage broker network around the nation to get consumers to apply for the loan. Once the loan has been approved (I use the word "approved" very loosely because very little due diligence is actually done by the so called lender), they are pre-placed into a REMIC. The lender then waits for the paperwork to be signed. Once it is signed, it is immediately transferred into the REMIC.

Once a REMIC has enough loans to be packaged, it then gets registered onto the SEC database and then gets converted and traded as a stock.

All the while, unbeknownst to the consumer, the lender all of a sudden switches their position from lender to servicer of the note. Again, as you recall under the accounting rule FAS 140... once an asset has been sold, the lender forever loses control of the asset. In other words, they no longer own or control your loan. They merely act as a servicer for your loan, with the proceeds going directly into the REMIC to be distributed to the shareholders.

Remember, since your lender is just a servicer, they do not own the note. They do not have the right to enforce the note. They can only act as a servicing agent.

Please refer to *CFR Title 12: Banks and Banking, Part 226 - Truth in Lending (Regulation Z)*. This is enclosed in the Appendix for your convenience. These are codified laws of banking. It defines who a Lender is, and what the rights of a Servicer are. Specifically, it refers in 226 (a) 1 that *a servicer is not treated as the owner of the obligation*.

> *(a) Scope. The disclosure requirements of this section apply to any covered person except as otherwise provided in this section. For purposes of this section:*
>
> *(1) A "covered person" means any person, as defined in §226.2(a)(22), that becomes the owner of an existing mortgage loan by acquiring legal title to the debt obligation, whether through a purchase, assignment, or other transfer, and who acquires more than one mortgage loan in any twelve-month period.* **For purposes of this section, a servicer of a mortgage loan shall not be treated as the owner of the obligation** *if the servicer holds title to the loan or it is assigned to the servicer solely for the administrative convenience of the servicer in servicing the obligation.*

You will also note that the scope does not cover the servicer if the servicer was assigned the note for administrative convenience in servicing the obligation.

This means, the servicer is not treated as and does not have the rights of a lender (or owner of the obligation).

As I discussed earlier, even if the servicer was to buy the note back after it has been securitized, reattachment of the loan/note to the Deed of Trust/Mortgage is impossible.

YOU CAN NOT MAKE CARROTS FROM CARROT JUICE

Once a loan has been written off, it is discharged. Once a loan has been securitized, reattachment is impossible.

Reattachment is impossible for the following reasons:

1) Permanent conversion

The promissory note has been converted into a stock as a permanent fixture. Its nature is forever changed. It is now and forever a stock. It is treated as a stock and governed as a stock under the SEC.

Since the Deed of Trust secures the promissory note, once the promissory note is destroyed, the Deed of Trust secures nothing. Therefore, the Trust is invalid.

2) Asset has been written off

Once an asset is written off, the debt is discharged since the owner of the asset has received compensation for the discharge in the form of tax credits from the IRS. The <u>debt has been settled</u>.

The servicer acts as a debt collector of an unsecured note. The servicer is deceiving the court, the county, and the borrower when it tries to re-attach the note to the Deed of Trust as if nothing has happened.

The funny thing about the law is, it is legal until or unless the other party objects. Since this scam is so devious, it is beyond the comprehension of most people...including that of lawyers and judges. It takes someone who has studied accounting, securities and law to unravel this deception. Most people in the legal profession only take the arguments on face value.

3) Broken chain of assignment

Under the Uniform Commercial Code (UCC), the promissory note is a one of a kind instrument. All assignments (much like endorsements on the back of a check) have to be done as a permanent fixture onto the original promissory note. The original promissory note has the only legally binding chain of title. Without a proper chain of title, the instrument is faulty.

Rarely can a lender "produce the note" because by law, the original note has to be destroyed. Remember? The note and the stock cannot exist at the same time. Oftentimes, the lender would come into court with a photocopy of the original note made years ago.

Another popular method of deceit lenders prefer is to use the State Civil Code in non-judicial states to state that "there is no law requiring a lender to produce the note or any other proof of claim." THEY DON'T HAVE IT and CANNOT PRODUCE IT.

Oftentimes, the lender would do blank assignments of the original promissory note into the REMIC. Then, when they need the note to perform the foreclosure, they will magically produce a blank assignment. Again, this is not legal and is bringing fraudulent documents before the courts and the county records.

Let's be very clear here. Once a loan has been securitized, **the note is no more**. Anything the lender brings to court as evidence is prima facie evidence of fraud. The attorney for the lender is either an accessory to fraud through ignorance or willful intent. Either way, as an informed borrower, it is your job to bring this deception to light so these lawyers can be sanctioned.

So, your lender would close your loan, sell it to a REMIC and get paid.

Once your loan goes into default, the loan is written off. The <u>loan is then bought by the servicer/lender as a dead/unsecured note</u>.

Once the servicer buys the dead note, they then claim to be the true holder in due course of a written off asset. They then present to the world that they are who they claim. They rely on the homeowner/borrower to be ignorant of this deception and clean up, allowing them to take possession of a house for pennies on the dollar.

This is the extent of the fraud done to the American public every single day.

As a homeowner defending your rights, it is imperative you understand the nature of this fraud so you can use these arguments to defend your home.

As a legal professional, it is imperative that you understand these arguments so you can raise the proper objections and interrogatories when representing your clients in a foreclosure defense.

LOAN MODS ARE A SCAM

By now, you should wise up to this whole notion of who is the real party of interest. So, if your lender is not a real and beneficial party of interest, how can they give you a loan mod?

The answer is...they can't.

"What? It happens all the time," I hear you say.

The truth is, very few loan modifications are approved and they usually take months.

If you have ever tried to talk to your bank about getting a loan mod, you will likely hear something like, "I am sorry sir, we can only consider you for a loan mod if you are 60 days or more delinquent."

WHAT??

That's just stupid.

Not really. Here's why.

Let's make it simpler for you to understand the scam. Remember FAS 140? Once an asset has been sold, the Lender/Servicer forever loses the right to enforce or control the asset...*except* when a loan is considered delinquent.

After 60 days, your servicer becomes a debt collector and is governed under the Fair Debt Collections Practices Act.

This is another scam they don't want you to know about.

If you have ever received a Notice of Default or anything else from the bank, you will see language like, "This is an attempt to collect a debt." This is required by law under the Fair Debt Collections Practices Act.

As we discussed earlier, typically, the REMIC writes the debt off to receive tax credit against future earnings. The servicer then buy this asset back as a **non-performing, non-secured debt**, very much like the collections agencies that buy non-performing credit card debts.

Once a debt has been written off for tax purposes, it is discharged. The company may sell the asset to a debt collector who will do anything and everything in its power to lie, cheat and steal to collect on the debt. This is why they must have the notice "This is an attempt to collect a debt." This is your clue that it is not an original creditor.

Once a debt is set off, the **FDIC comes in and covers 80% of the face value of the loan.**

Your bank then buys the bad debt for pennies on the dollar from the REMIC so that they can negotiate a loan modification.

Once they get you to sign the loan mod agreement, they have successfully renegotiated, recontracted and re-acquired the loan. Notice how hard it is to get a loan modification? Do you know why?

They can no longer dump their toxic assets on those "suckers on Wall Street." *Fool me once,* shame on you. *Fool me twice, shame on me.* Wall Street is getting wise. Now, strict underwriting standards must be applied because they have to keep the loan.

Furthermore, there are strict accounting rules about buying back toxic assets. The asset has to be bought on the open market. That is why it takes months for them to buy your note back.

Can you see the light now? Are you having an "aha" moment?

But If They Bought the Loan, Don't they then Have the Right to Foreclose?

Once a debt has been written off as a bad debt, the owners get tax credits for the asset. When this happens, the debt is discharged. Settled. Gone.

What these banks are doing is buying a discharged asset. They then try to convince the world; the borrower, the courts, and the Trustee, that they are the real party of interest. That is a lie.

As I discussed earlier, once a loan has been written off, it cannot be re-adhered and made whole again. Remember? **You cannot make carrots from carrot juice**. It's forever changed.

Enter Robo-Signers and Fraudulent Loan Assignments

Let me ask you a question. If you could pick up a promissory note for pennies on the dollar, and all you have to do is to "convince" (con) the homeowners that you are the true party of interest...to what extent would you go to lie/cheat/steal to get the home?

The answer is...**whatever it takes**. At least that's what the banks are doing.

This brings us back to the Uniform Commercial Code. Under the law, the original promissory note is the only valid and legally binding chain of title for the note. Your original promissory note is like an original check. It's a one of a kind instrument.

To convince the court that they have the right to foreclose, banks have taken to:

a) Forging documents
b) Creating arbitrary loan assignments to suit their needs
c) Bringing fraudulent documents before the court
d) Recording fraudulent documents at the county

There is a company called Loan Processing Services (LPS), who for less than $100, can fabricate any loan documents the bank needs to facilitate their foreclosure. It's called reverse engineering of title. Instead of following proper legal due process of proper chain of title assignment as required by law, these companies will reverse engineer a title to facilitate for the foreclosure, even if they have to bend the rules a little. _They then go under oath to testify that they have first hand knowledge of the fact that these loan documents are legitimate._

I have depositions of employees from these foreclosure mills passing the notary stamp around and stamping signatures as they go. They literally pass around notary signatures like they are a rubber stamp. Often times, you can see signatures as notaries that do not match those registered with the State.

There was even an instance where one outfit had an "assignment table" where they would put a whole stack of paper and a manager would then rubber stamp the appropriate loan assignment as they saw fit with no verification, no firsthand knowledge of the fact, no confirmation, zip.

But as I discussed earlier, you cannot make carrots from carrot juice. If a loan has been securitized, any supposed original promissory note is nothing more than counterfeit at best; not to mention securities fraud.

Don't believe us? Just go to Youtube and search for the <u>Alan Grayson Foreclosure Fraud</u> and the <u>video deposition of nationwide title clearing bryan bly</u>. These are but two of hundreds of such videos. Congressman Grayson is a Representative from Florida...one of the worst affected States in the US.

It's enough to make you sick.

CHAPTER 4:
LEGAL ARGUMENTS

The issues around foreclosures are confusing, stressful and emotional.

This is made worst because the banks are committing open fraud but are trying to cover it up. Like I mentioned earlier, not even the bank's managers or their own counsel knows what's going on. By reading this book, you are more educated than 99% of the people out there facing foreclosure.

Take a read of these two great articles:

http://www.usatoday.com/money/economy/housing/2010-12-21-mortgagenote21_CV_N.htm

http://www.bloomberg.com/news/2011-01-06/foreclosures-may-be-undone-by-massachusetts-ruling-on-mortgage-transfers.html

And another great article from the Financial Times about Securitization:

http://ftalphaville.ft.com/blog/2011/01/07/452081/a-court-case-to-challenge-securitisation-standards/

With your newfound set of eyes, read the articles again. Seriously, click on the link and read it. You will now be able to spot the lies and say "aha" when you look at the problem through the loan fraud lens. It all makes sense.

Everyone is confused. The lawyers and the judges think that it's just a procedural error. It's not.

In this chapter I will go into more legal arguments to discuss the issue of subject matter jurisdiction (or Standing) as well as the Fair Debt Collections Practices Act as it applies to the foreclosure problem.

BEYOND "SHOW ME THE NOTE"

Some of you may have heard of the argument "show me the note." Time and time again, these cases are tossed out of court. This scheme comes from well-intentioned people in the media who are ill-informed about the legal process.

Fundamental to the American jurisprudence system is the concept of standing.

Let me illustrate standing using another analogy.

Let's say a husband and wife are arguing in court over who should take the couch. All of a sudden, some guy shows up and says, "I want the couch." This third party is not a real party of interest and therefore has no standing to be in the controversy.

However, if that third party then shows up with a sales receipt from the wife proving that he paid for the couch, all of a sudden he has standing.

This is really important for us to understand. In building your case, you should study up on the securitization process and arguments. You have to be able to articulate and defend your allegation that the bank is not a real party of interest, and therefore, lacks subject matter jurisdiction on the controversy. In other words, **they lack standing**.

Under the *Federal Rules of Civil Procedure Rule 17*, "an action must be pursued by a real party of interest." (Google it up.) So, if it can be proven that the bank is not a real party of interest, then the bank cannot enforce the note. Don't take our word for it. Look it up yourself and consult counsel.

One of the ways a bank can obfuscate the problems of securitization is to present "the note" to the court. As I explained above, the note is invalid once it has been securitized, but, in order for the bank to perpetrate the theft of your house, they will do whatever it takes to complete the scam.

Under Uniform Commercial Code, a note is a one of a kind negotiable instrument that has the only legally binding chain of assignment. Oftentimes, your lender will show up with a photocopy of the note made years ago…again, obscuring the facts in order to steal your house. This is admissible unless you know how to object. Again, consult with counsel about the *Federal Rules of Evidence 1002 and 1003*.

Another way banks hide their fraud is to do what's called "blank assignments" so that the loan may be assigned many times amongst themselves that are tracked by MERS (which I will explain later), while keeping a blank assignment of the note handy in the event a foreclosure is needed. This is blatant abuse of the law. The law is very specific here. The promissory note as well as the Deed of Trust must be together at all times and there must always be a clear and unambiguous chain of title that is traceable in public records for all parties of interest in real estate.

Remember, the argument we want to go by is not "show me the note," but instead "show me standing" or "show me that you are a real party of interest." One of the ways they can do this is to present the original promissory note. By understanding the argument of securitization, you may be able to refute the note.

THE DEED OF TRUST AND MORTGAGE

When you sign to close on your loan, you signed a number of documents. Most importantly are the Deed of Trust or Mortgage (depending what State you live in) and the Promissory note.

The Deed of Trust/Mortgage secures the promissory note.

The Deed of Trust/Mortgage is the document that gives your lender the right to sell your house in a foreclosure action

Both the Deed of Trust/Mortgage and the Promissory note must always point to the same party at all times to have Perfection of Chain of Title.

BIFURCATION

In every State (that I know of), the law is very specific in regards to recordation of public record at the County Hall of Records with regards to real property. Specifically all real parties of interest in real property must be recorded at the County. In other words, if someone has an interest in a piece of property, they **MUST** record this interest on public record.

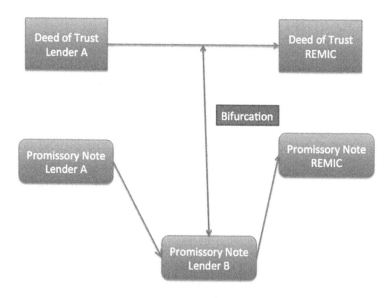

When a promissory note is sold or assigned, it therefore must be recorded in public record to maintain perfected chain of title for the security.

If there is a break in a chain of title, then **bifurcation** occurs where the Deed of Trust/Mortgage points to one party, while the promissory note points to another party.

Carpenter v Longan

Under a US Supreme Court ruling, it is stated that the Promissory Note is the object, and the Deed of Trust is the attachment.

Where the Promissory note goes, the Deed of Trust must follow, much like a dog and the tail. Where the dog goes, the tail must follow. Not the other way round.

Once bifurcation occurs, then the security has been broken because State law has been violated.

VIOLATION OF APPLICABLE STATE LAW

In every Deed of Trust/Mortgage, it states specifically that the instrument is subject to applicable State and Federal laws. If it can be shown that an assignment of the promissory note occurs without the corresponding assignment at the county recorder's office for the Deed of Trust/Mortgage, then the instrument has violated State law. Thus, violating the terms of the Deed of Trust/Mortgage, making the instrument invalid.

Since interest in the promissory note has been sold to a REMIC (Real Estate Mortgage Investment Conduit) and proper assignment was never done at the county, then the terms of the Deed of Trust/Mortgage has been violated, **making it invalid**. This will convert the debt from a **secured** instrument **to an unsecured instrument**. This means the lender might be able to sue you to collect the money, but can never sell your property to collect on the collateral.

However, this happens every day right in front of our eyes because the general public is too uninformed to argue these points and so the banks get away with this.

The lender can not enforce an instrument that is defective.

PERFECTION OF CHAIN OF TITLE

In January 2011, the Massachusetts Supreme Court issued a decision in U.S. BANK NATIONAL ASSOCIATION vs. Antonio IBANEZ in which all the Justices unanimously agreed. In order for the bank to be able to foreclose, they must show a perfection of chain of title both in the Deed of Trust/Mortgage and the Promissory note. It was also ruled that a blank assignment was not acceptable proof of perfection of title for the promissory note.

This is HUGE. You should be referring to this case and Motion the court to take "mandatory judicial notice" for the ruling decision in your case if you are considering doing any sort of litigation whether as a defendant in a Judicial State or as a Plaintiff in a Non-Judicial State.

Here are the important points you need to understand from this Supreme Court decision:

1) A Defective Title cannot be fixed.

The Massachusetts Supreme Court ruled that the bank has to demonstrate perfection of title at the time the Notice of Default is issued.

A defective title is like bad food. Once food has gone bad, you can never fix it. The same goes with the Deed of Trust/Mortgage. The "lender" can not retro sign or "reverse engineer" the Chain of Title after the fact. This is the case most of the time when the case is handled by a foreclosure mill. They have robo-signers whose job is to sign bogus assignments and reverse engineer titles.

It is your job to challenge this point when your lender presents supposed "proof" before the court. Oftentimes, they will bring in a photocopy of the Deed of Trust made years ago at the time you closed on your loan. The photocopy does not and **can not attest to who the current real and beneficiary party of interest is.**

2) The Bank must show a perfection of the Chain of Title for the Deed of Trust/Mortgage

This means that any assignments of the Promissory note must also be reflected at the county recorder's office (and not with MERS - I will talk about MERS in a bit).

If an assignment of the Promissory Note is not recorded on the County Records, then perfection is not achieved.

What this means is, if you can prove that your note has been securitized or sold to another party away from your original lender, and you can prove that they did not record this assignment at the County Recorder's Office, then bifurcation occurred. This leads to a defect in the chain of title, making the Deed of Trust/Mortgage unenforceable.

3) The Bank must show a perfection of the Chain of Title for the Promissory Note

If we have a situation where you closed with Bank A, and Bank A sold the note to Bank B, who then sold the note to a REMIC (securitized the note), then it was ruled that there must be a chain of endorsement following Uniform Commercial Code § 9-206. Typically, this is done in the form of a stamp on the back of the promissory note from Bank A to Bank B as "Pay to the Order of Bank B Without Recourse".

Title must show this chain of "Pay to the Order of" on the back of the note, just like it would on a check, all the way to the last person trying to collect on the note. If the bank cannot show this chain of title ending in appoint it as the person on the title, it does not have perfection of title, and is not eligible to collect.

In order to collect and enforce the note under UCC § 9-301, the party enforcing the note must demonstrate that it has the position of Holder in Due Course or having authority from the Holder. Failing that, the bank is committing theft.

4) Blank Assignments are Not Acceptable

It is STANDARD BANK PRACTICE to make blank assignments to avoid the problem of having to maintain proper chain of title on the promissory note. In previous situations, the courts have allowed blank assignment and possession to be acceptable form of proof of claim.

With the Massachusetts Supreme Court ruling, this is no longer true. Blank assignments are no longer acceptable forms of proof of Perfection.

Let me repeat this if you missed it.

If your note has been securitized, then the bank that is handling the securitization ALWAYS create a Blank Assignment to be used in the event a foreclosure action is initiated and proof of title needs to be produced. All they do is to give the blank assignment promissory note to the party wishing to foreclose and viola!

With your newfound knowledge, you now know how to build an objection to this practice.

If you refer to point 1), the bank cannot reverse engineer these assignments. Once the instrument is defective, it is forever defective. Proper assignment must be done in conjunction and at the time of the deed, not retrospectively.

All paper work must be demonstrated to be perfected at the time of the Notice of Default. If it can be shown that this is not the case, then you could have the foreclosure process thrown out.

WHO OR WHAT IS MERS?

In order to facilitate the tracking of the thousands of true shareholders who owns the promissory note, an electronic registration system must be developed. Bankers got together and created the Mortgage Electronic Registration Systems (MERS). As you can see from our previous arguments that due to IRS Code 860 governing tax pass through for Special Purpose Vehicles, the real parties of interest are the individual shareholders. This could be thousands of them... and it would be impossible to track these parties at the County Record. Furthermore, these parties change hands literally daily, so it would be impossible to track these using conventional means.

When you look at your Deed of Trust or Mortgage, if your loan mentioned MERS of the first or second page, then there is a good chance (100% actually) that your loan has been securitized.

MERS functions as a registry. Much like your County Recorder. However, what is unique about MERS is they are often named either as a Beneficiary or a Nominee on the Deed of Trust/Mortgage. There are a number of problems with this.

   a) To be a Beneficiary, one has to put up the money to fund the loan. MERS never fronted up a single dim for the loan. They are solely there for the purpose of tracking transfers.

b) MERS recordation is not official. The only legally recognized recordation on public record is with the County.

c) MERS is never a Holder in Due Course. No promissory note was ever assigned to them.

d) Only a real and beneficiary party of interest may assign a promissory note, appoint a substitution of trustee or assign the Deed of Trust.

MERS appoints loan assignments to mysterious parties every day for the purpose of foreclosure without actually having the authority to do so. If you have ever received a Notice of Default or Notice of Substitution of Trustee, you will likely see MERS appointing some entity you've never heard of or dealt with as the beneficiary of your Deed of Trust/Mortgage.

Courts all around the country have ruled against MERS having the authority to appoint Trustees and assign Deeds of Trust/Mortgages. Unless it is officially registered at the County Hall of Records, it is not officially recognized.

It makes as much sense as your local County Recorder going in, taking the Deed to your house and assigning it to his brother. He has no authority to do so.

The Recorder is just that...a keeper of record. He cannot appoint anyone to be anything. MERS functions just like a recorder. It is a registration system. It too does not have the authority to appoint anyone. MERS is not a real or beneficial party of interest. This has been validated in many Federal court decisions.

On your Deed of Trust/Mortgage, you will see language that says "From time to time, the Lender may appoint a Substitution of Trustee...", no where does it say "The Nominee or the Beneficiary may....". Only the Lender can do this. Yet MERS blatantly violates the terms of the Deed of Trust every single day.

The Terms of a Deed of Trust is like an "Article of Incorporation" or Constitution of your Trust, much like the Constitution of the United States. It is the underlying terms that binds the whole Trust together, and must not be violated.

So when we have a situation where State law is being violated through improper assignment, the Deed of Trust is made invalid. When the Trustee is being appointed by "some party" that is not given the proper authority to do so, this also casts issue to make the Deed of Trust defective.

THE ISSUE OF A DEFECTIVE INSTRUMENT

If the promissory note is owned by thousands of parties, then there is no one party that may come forth to lay claim on the promissory note. If no one party can be named "the beneficiary" or "the lender", then the promissory note is defective.

If no loan assignment was properly done, it cannot be "fixed". A lender cannot simply reverse engineer the title of the Deed of Trust or Promissory note to make it better. Once an instrument is defective, it cannot be used to collect the debt.

If the terms of the Deed of Trust/Mortgage can be shown to violate applicable State law, then it too is defective. If it is defective, then it cannot be used to give the lender the "due on sale" clause. The terms of the Deed of Trust must be respected in whole and one cannot pick and choose which part to respect and which part to ignore.

You have to understand how to read the terms of the Deed of Trust/Mortgage so you can articulate and defend your title against fraudulent claims. So, I would recommend that you bring out your Mortgage/Deed of Trust from your closing packet and take a careful look at them to see if there are any of the above defects I mentioned. You might be surprised at what you discover.

ROBO-SIGNERS AND DOCUMENT FABRICATION

What banks have done to correct these defects in their documentation is to do what's called "reverse engineer" the title. As you recall, they are required by law to do the assignments within a reasonable time of the deed, but in their haste to make money, these things were conveniently overlooked.

There are now even outfits that banks would go to to fabricate the required documents, complete with affidavits (from a minimum wage employee who does not even work for the bank) to testify that the bank has standing to foreclose. As you can see from the price list below, it's amazingly affordable.

GETNET™ RATE SHEET

XCODE	SERVICE	AMOUNT
INF1	Obtain PIN Number from Online Public Records	$6.60 + SH
IA03	Create Missing Intervening Assignment	$35.00 + TPC
IA04	Record Prepared Assignments	$12.95 + TPC
IA05	Cure Defective Assignment	$12.95 + TPC
IS01	FHA and VA Mortgage Insurance Submission	$95.00 + TPC
UC01	Retrieving a UCC Package	$15.95 + TPC
CF01	Recreate Entire Collateral File	$95.00 + TPC

The rule regarding an affidavit is that one has to be done with first hand knowledge of the facts. These minimum wage employees process between 100 to 200 files a day. They literally rubberstamp these documents with absolutely no verification whatsoever of the facts. There have been instances where several banks try to foreclose on the same house...yet these document mills have employees creating affidavits to testify that they know for a fact that the loan belongs to the foreclosing entity. Someone is lying. We just don't know who.

That's why we have what's called "the due process of the law". When one makes an affidavit, one is declaring under oath that one is telling the truth and knows that their statements are accurate with first hand knowledge. How can one know with first hand knowledge of the facts when one process 100+ files a day? It's impossible.

If you take a look at the price list above, you can see that for around $35, literally anyone can order the documents to fabricate a missing assignment of the chain of title to demonstrate to the court that the party doing the foreclosing has the authority to do so.

As we mentioned in the previous section, a defective instrument is like bad food. Once it is defective, it can not be fixed.

If you get a MSI (Mortgage Scene Investigation) securitization audit, it will likely show that your loan is subject to robo-signing. This can then be used as a valid legal defense to prove that the assignments were not done legally following proper due process.

ILLEGAL TRUSTEE ARGUMENT

There's been two instances in which a Federal Court Judge issued a Statewide injunction freezing all foreclosures against homeowners against Bank of America and Recontrust. One in Utah in late 2010, and more recently in January 2011 in Nevada because in both instances, Recontrust is not registered to do business in that State.

If a company wants to do business in a State, it need to register within that State as an entity. This way, if someone within that State wants to sue them, they can look up who the owners are, and where they live so they can be properly served with a summons.

In almost all instances, these foreclosure mills are not registered to do business in the State they are attempting to foreclose in.

Many homeowners have used this defense to at least forestall foreclosure. It is not enough to stop a foreclosure, but it is another claim the homeowner can make in a Quiet Title Action defense making the argument that the Trustee is a "non-entity".

THE RECONVEYANCE ARGUMENT

This strategy comes from an attorney in California who is doing this with his own house.

If you look at your Deed of Trust or Mortgage, you will invariably see language that covers the clause of "reconveyance". The language typically goes like this:

> "23. Reconveyance. Upon payment of all sums secured by this Security Instrument, Lender shall request Trustee to reconvey the Property and shall surrender this Security Instrument and all notes evidencing debt secured by this security agreement to trustee."

When you have a situation where:

a) The note can be proven that it was securitized, then it can be proven that the lender has in fact been paid in full.

b) The note has been sold from Bank A, to Bank B, and then to Bank C who is trying to foreclose.

In any event, this strategy involves bringing a civil action against the Originator; Bank A, requiring them to do their job in a breach of contract civil action.

You see, a Deed of Trust secures the promissory note. It is the Deed of Trust that gives the Lender the "power of sale" clause to foreclose. If the original lender is forced to issue a reconveyance, then the Deed of Trust is collapsed.

This is a very effective yet easy method some people have used to stop foreclosure. Reason being that:

a) The Originator is often out of business and can not respond to the civil action, thus the homeowner wins by default.

b) The Originator had already sold the note with "no recourse". This means, the REMIC or the servicer can NEVER go back to the Originator

c) If the Originator loses the civil action by default, nothing bad happens to them.

d) If the Originator wins the civil action, nothing good happens to them.

Here's the kicker. If the Originator is still in business, and they lose the civil action in court, then there are very specific dire consequences that results. If they lose, then it can be proven that every loan they have ever originated that has lost their home is the result of their gross negligence to perform their duty. This means every homeowner who has lost his or her home can sue the Originator.

It is for this reason that the Originator often doesn't show up, or settles when confronted with this strategy.

If you are interested more about this strategy, we have a sample kit that will guide you through the process on our site at:

www.consumerdefenseprograms.com. Look under the Products tab for the "Quick Reconveyance Method".

THE FAIR DEBT COLLECTIONS PRACTICES ACT

As you recalled, your pretender lender becomes a debt collector after you are 60 days delinquent. This is the only way they can negotiate a loan modification with you because it gets discharged out of the REMIC. I have included a copy of the FDCPA in the Appendix at the end of this book. You can also simply Google "Fair Debt Collections Practices Act"

Let's talk a bit more about debt collectors. It is a scam. Debt collectors depend on people's ignorance to collect their ill-gotten gains. This is one of those dirty little secrets bankers have been hiding for years. They don't want you to know this scam. I am blowing their dirty laundry out in the open because I am sick of seeing so many people suffer at the hands of bankers.

As I pointed out earlier using the analogy of the farmer, it is in the interest of the creditor to write off the debt.

A debt collector is someone who (is not the original creditor) buys a debt that has been offsetted, and attempts to collect it. This is very important for you to understand. This is why the government created a set of laws called the Fair Debt Collections Practices Act (USC Title 15 Section 1692) in order to minimize the deceit and protect people. Sadly, not many lawyers understand this mechanic. They think debt collectors act legitimately.

Let's say it again. Once a debt has been written off, **it is discharged**. It cannot be collected again. Debt collectors use deception to convince people that they were assigned the debt.

So, how does this relate to a REMIC and a debt collector? As I discussed earlier, the individual shareholders are the real and beneficial interest holders. Since the individual shareholders cannot endorse and assign their portion of the loss, **then they have to write it off as a bad debt**. The Trustee of the REMIC cannot do it neither because the Trustee is not the real and beneficial holder of the promissory note. The REMIC has given up that right when it chose to structure itself as a Special Purpose Vehicle (SPV) for the purpose of a straight tax pass through.

The only way your lender can foreclose on you is that they rely on the same deception tactics used by debt collectors. The Fair Debt Collections Practices Act governs the deceptive practices also. Remember, a debt collector pulls off their deception through people's ignorance. *This is what your "lender" is doing to you.* That is why in all their communication, you will see "This is an attempt to collect a debt". An original creditor is not required to disclose this.

So if you are in a court or if you are counsel representing your client, it is important for you to ask opposing counsel to stipulate the nature of their ownership of the note. Oftentimes, opposing counsel will come into the court room representing that their client has "repurchased the note", not realizing that they have in fact brought fraud before the court. If opposing counsel is ignorant, then they are not lying. It is up to you to get them to stipulate the true nature of the negotiable instrument through interrogatories and discovery; including subpoena of accounting records. If you do this, watch how quickly the blood drains from opposing counsel's face. It's quite a sight.

A defective instrument is not enforceable. An instrument that has been previously discharged and bought as a bad debt is not enforceable. **Don't be fooled**. It's like buying a cheap knock off Rolex watch in Mexico. It might look the same, but underneath the face, it is not.

THE DEBT VALIDATION LETTER

Let's analyze the Fair Debt Collections Practices Act, and specifically the portion governing the validation of debt. Under USC Title 15 Section 1692(g), you are entitled to ask a debt collector for the validation of the debt. Upon dispute of the debt, all collection activities must cease until the debt collector can validate the debt. Sadly, the consumer has only 30 days to dispute the debt or else they admit to the debt.

If you have received a Notice of Default (NOD) from your "lender", you will see that there is language specifically that says "If you do not dispute this debt within 30 days, then you admit to owing this debt." Go on. Go grab your letter and take a good look.

If you have not received a Notice of Default letter (or if you have received it within 30 days), you can still send a Notice of Debt validation letter to your "lender" to dispute the debt. I have included a sample NOD Dispute letter on http://www.consumerdefenseprograms.com.

However, this does not mean you waive your rights to challenge your lender if you are more than 30 days past default. You can still do it. You can write your lender and your Trustee (in a non-Judicial State) demanding that they produce proof of claim under the FDCPA under USC Title 15 Section 1692(g). Your "lender" is required to respond within 30 days. Failure to do so results in a violation of the FDCPA which carries a penalty of up to $1000 per violation (you simply have to sue them to collect). The FDCPA also has special damage provisions for class actions. 15 U.S.C. §1692k. Recovery of statutory damages for the class is limited to 1% of the debt collector's net worth or $500,000, whichever is less.

You will know when the debt collector doesn't have the note when a response is sent back giving the Borrower either a "We don't recognize your request" or stating the information is

"Proprietary". Don't let them get away with that. The FDCPA rules are clear! In most cases, the Lender/ Servicer will send you anything but the items requested. Most of the time, debt collectors will send the following:

- Some papers printed from a computer, not sure what they are
- Nothing certified (notarized) and especially not dated recently
- Nothing showing the name and signature of the original lender or past note holder
- Nothing proving the notification of a transfer
- Simple copies of some kind of billing statement etc.

All of which are unacceptable! The Lenders, Servicers and Debt Collectors **ABSOLUTELY know what the legal requirements are**. They will challenge anyone who disputes a debt to see if you know the law. This is why this is so important for you to know what the law are as well!

Under the **Uniform Commercial Code Section 3-204**, the name and the signature of both the beneficiary and the original creditor must be disclosed in the same document § 3-204 (d). The signature of the borrower must be included as well into the assignment or transfer; unless a clause in the deed of trust/mortgage waives that (most deeds of trust disclose this at clause #20).

FTC, HUD COMPLAINT and Comptroller of the Currency

If you believe your mortgage servicer has not responded appropriately to a written inquiry, you should contact your State's **Attorney General Consumer Protection Office**. You should also should contact the **Department of Housing and Urban Development** (HUD) to file a complaint under the RESPA regulations.

It is important that you issue complaints to these authorities because they can not act on their own. They need a damaged party to give them the authority to prosecute a case. The more people complain to these authorities, the more likely they will take notice and investigate.

In your complaint, explain to them what you have asked, provide copies of your communication and where they broke the law. Specifically, under the Fair Debt Collections Debt Section 1692g.

Write to:

Office of RESPA and Interstate Land Sales,

Department of Housing and Urban Development,

451 Seventh Street, S.W., Room 9154,

Washington, DC 20410,

You might also want to contact the Federal Trade Commission (FTC). The FTC works for the consumer to prevent fraudulent, deceptive, and unfair business practices in the marketplace and to provide information to help consumers spot, stop, and avoid them.

The FTC's address is:
600 Pennsylvania Avenue, NW
Washington, DC 20580
(202) 326-2222
www.ftc.gov

You should also write to the Office of Comptoller of the Currency. This is the organization that oversees banking and banking practices.

You can write to the Office of the Comptroller of the Currency at:

Comptroller of the Currency
Administrator of National Banks
Washington, DC 20219
http://www.occ.gov/

CHAPTER 5:
WHAT ABOUT MY DEBT OBLIGATIONS?

"But I have been brought up to be honorable. I am a man of my word. I signed the promissory note, promising that I would pay. I got my house. I am now in default. The bank has the right to foreclose on my house..."

Most of us are decent, honest folks. We believe in paying our debts. Millions and millions of people echo the above sentiment. You are not alone.

<u>I am not talking about a free lunch.</u>

I am not talking about scamming the system, nor am I talking about taking advantage of some bizarre loophole in the law.

What I am talking about is fairness, equity and giving the everyday homeowner a fair shake.

HEADS I WIN, TAILS I WIN

The beauty with the capitalist system is that it encourages free enterprise. It encourages people to take risks. With high risks come high rewards. Oftentimes you win, and sometimes you lose.

However, in the situation where "heads I win (and keep all the money), tails I get bailed out"...it gets down to a question of fairness and equity. Remember, the bailout comes from taxpayer money (YOUR MONEY). They received over 3.5 TRILLION dollars of free money. Pretty much with no strings attached, to do with as they see fit.

On the other side of the spectrum, millions of homeowners are being kicked out of their homes. No loan modifications to compensate for being "upside down" (i.e., they owe more than their house is worth).

Where's the fairness in that? Particularly when they can use that same bailout money to pay their top executives millions in bonuses (for the number of homes they can foreclose and how quickly they can process them).

I don't know about you, but this sort of behavior is enough for the pitchforks to come out.

Enough is enough.

BEING PAID NOT ONCE, BUT AT LEAST 3 TIMES

Being in a capitalist society, making money is not only OK, but is encouraged. But where does making a profit end and extortion/greed begin?

1) The Banks Risked None of Their Own Money

One of the rules of capitalism is risk vs. rewards. With high risks come high rewards. If they were able to create money out of thin air (through the fractional reserve banking system) and make 2.5 times the face value of a loan...I am talking about 10,000% return on cash. This is an awesome return. Sign me up any day.

2) The Bank Got Paid When They Securitized The Loan

As I discussed, they got paid between 1.05 to 1.5 times the face value of the loan when they securitized...within days of closing your loan.

3) They Got Paid for Stock Value Appreciation

The Lender also owns stock in the REMICS. They can own up to 10% of these Trusts. So when the market went up, they profited from the appreciation of the asset.

4) They Got Paid by TARP

They got paid over 3.5 TRILLION dollars of taxpayer money to do as they see fit, including buying up other banks.

5) They Got Paid by FDIC

When the loan goes into default, banks are covered for 70% to 80% of the value of the loan.

6) They Were Covered By Mortgage Insurance

In addition to being covered by FDIC, often times, homebuyers are forced to buy mortgage insurance to cover the event of a mortgage default. When the homeowner defaults on a loan, the bank was paid by mortgage insurance.

7) They Get to Keep Your House

To add insult to injury, they also get to kick you out of your home. Keep the house and sell it again to the next sucker so they can repeat the scam.

How many times are these guys paid? Where is the fairness in all this for the average little guy?

I don't know about you, but I am tired of being screwed. No one ever looks after the little guy.

This is why I wrote this book in the hopes that you will share it with your friends and neighbors so more Americans can wake up to this scam.

I am sure there are some people who disagree with what we are saying. But thank God, that's still legal in this country. We each have the right to our own opinion.

All I am saying is, enough is enough.

When they threaten our homes, they threaten our families. The home is one of our most sacred assets. Without it, we are lost. Once they own our homes, they can use that to leverage us and further enslave us.

The bankers have backed us into a no win situation. I hope that by educating you about this scam, you will decide to fight back.

CHAPTER 6:
THE BLOODY ROAD AHEAD

By all indications, 2011 and onwards will be even worse than before. More and more loans known as option ARMs (adjustable rate mortgages) will come due as many of these loans have a romance period of 3 to 5 years. Once these come due, and people's interest rates get hiked up, more people will get into trouble with their loans.

As of the middle of 2010, the general American public started learning about robo-signers and improper loan assignments. This has been all over the news. But, as you have seen, this deceit goes much deeper than just procedural errors. It is massive and willful fraud committed by the banking cartel.

It is anticipated that there will be a massive boom in the legal profession in the next 5 to 10 years in the area of foreclosure defense and litigation, because as more and more homeowners learn about loan fraud, they will likely seek out legal professionals to seek relief from our predatory friends in the banking industry.

Not only that, there will be more and more homeowners who have already lost their homes wanting to have their grievances redressed as they discover that their foreclosure was done fraudulently. There is no statute of limitations on fraud. This will mean more and more lawyers will have plenty of opportunities to pursue civil actions against these lenders for real and punitive damages.

This is a problem that will haunt the banking industry for years to come. I expect there will be a massive rise in advertising across the nation for "wrongful foreclosure contingency attorneys" in which attorneys will pursue clients who have lost their homes due to fraud for a big chunk of the settlement.

This is why the people in the know in the banking industry are doing everything they can to keep the truth from coming out. This problem will result in very significant and long lasting implications to the banking industry for years to come.

THE COLLAPSE OF THE BANKING INDUSTRY?

If homeowners around the country start awakening to the fraud committed and start suing banks en mass, could this lead to a collapse of the banking industry?

As much as I dislike the fraud that is being committed by our banking buddies, I do not relish the thought of the collapse of the banking industry. It's like a child behaving badly. I disapprove of the poor behavior, but I do not dislike the child.

Let's not forget that we in the Western world have a lot to be grateful for thanks to our banking friends. Much of our current luxury and way of life is, in part, due to the banking system.

A collapse of the banking system will hurt everyone and ruin any chance of economic recovery.

That said, Congress would never let this happen. There will likely be additional free bail out monies issued to cover our banking friends against any possible harm done to them. As we recall, they are simply "too big to fail" and beyond reproach. They hold too much sway in government and fund most of the political contributions to our representatives.

FREE LUNCH FOR HOMEOWNERS?

Another argument I have heard is that this is just another way for deadbeat homeowners to get away with a free lunch and "stick it to the banks" at the expense of other homeowners who pay their dues "like everybody else."

Nothing can be further from the truth.

Most people who cannot afford to pay for their mortgages are people who have lost their jobs as a result of the economy. Bad things sometimes happen to good people. This does not make them bad people. These are your friends, your neighbors, or your relatives who are suffering.

The grievances we want to address are:

1) The housing bubble was caused by the banking industry out of greed
2) The banks have enjoyed record profits from the boom
3) The banks have been paid by Wall Street as well as by taxpayer money
4) The banks are not the real parties of interest in foreclosure actions

5) The notes bought from the secondary markets are unsecured. Re-adhesion of an asset that has been written off is illegal, immoral and unconscionable.

6) Haven't the people suffered enough?

The point is, even if every homeowner decides to stop paying their mortgages, the lenders are not harmed directly because they are nothing but a servicer. The people who are potentially harmed are the shareholders of the REMICs. But their losses are covered by the FDIC. The banks have the TARP money set aside for this purpose. <u>They have already been covered for this loss</u>.

The **law is the law**. Banks cannot pick and choose which laws to use when it is convenient for them, and which laws to ignore when it isn't. They cannot reattach an unsecured note (that has been written off), and con the homeowners into thinking that it is *Perfect* (without defects).

What these so called lenders (servicers) are doing is actually taking this opportunity to reap massive profits by acquiring people's houses for very little. They will then manipulate the market again to re-stimulate the economy and wait for the prices of these houses to rise so they can sell them for even more profits.

I feel this is unethical and repugnant. All I am saying is, enough is enough.

What I am saying is that the fraud must stop. **<u>A foreclosure action must be done by a real party of interest</u>**. Period. If it isn't, then it is nothing more than theft and extortion.

OPPORTUNITY FOR PEACE

I hope that by awakening more and more homeowners and people in the legal profession of the extent of loan fraud that our banking friends might decide to come clean.

All we are asking is a fair deal. People all around the country are suffering. All we're saying is, enough is enough. Let the greed stop and let the compassion for each other begin.

I hope to avoid the blood bath of litigation ahead as it will not be good for the banking industry and ultimately, it will come back to haunt everyone. Like I said, we need a strong and reliable banking system.

I hope that banks will feel that they can come back to homeowners and proactively renegotiate home loans to make housing more affordable for everyone to keep people in their homes.

If the people in the banking industry can see that they are exposed to a massive amount of litigation damages if they continue with this fraud and change their predatory ways, perhaps we might see some economic recovery as more people can actually afford to stay in their homes and spend money to support the economy instead of feeding the banking system.

I hope that the people, the media, the government and the banks can all work out an amicable accord to allow homeowners to stay in their homes. If not, then this country is heading towards a legal blood bath.

CHAPTER 7:
WHAT ARE MY OPTIONS?

The purpose of this book is to share some information with you. I hope that this is just the beginning of your educational journey.

Again, please don't believe a word I say. Do your own research.

Whatever you do, don't go to your bank manager and demand justice. He is likely to be as ignorant as everyone else. This is a scheme that only a few people at the highest level of the banking and finance industry are aware of.

Don't go in half-cocked and demand that your bank show you that they are a real party of interest. Arm yourself with more information.

If this book has inspired you to take action, then the next step is for you to learn more about this process so you can properly articulate and defend yourself.

If you are facing foreclosure, time is not on your side. Playing the ostrich game of hiding your head in the sand is not going to make the problem go away. The banks are going to steal your home and kick your family to the curb.

I understand that many of you facing foreclosure are facing crippling depression so that it is a struggle to even wake up and get dressed every day. I know. I have been there.

But really, your choices **are very simple**.

Option 1. Give up. Continue to feel sorry for yourself. Wallow in your depression. Lose your home.

Option 2. Learn to fight. Defend your rights. Educate yourself. Force your lender to prove standing.

If you are inclined to learn more and educate yourself further, I've put together a series of videos to help you get up to speed quickly about foreclosure defense. People have paid a lot of money to come to our seminars (including lawyers) to learn this information. I've invested thousands and thousands of hours researching this information so you can cut to the chase. Like I said, if you are facing foreclosure, time is not on your side.

To learn more about foreclosure defense strategies, come to:

http://www.consumerdefenseprograms.com/resources/videos/

DO YOUR OWN RESEARCH

If you are interested in fighting foreclosure, then you need to arm yourself with more information. Do not rely on the information contained in this book. This book should be used as a starting point and a framework only.

Verify the facts. **<u>Don't believe a word I say</u>**. Consider this a work of fiction. Discover your own truth. Seriously, I could be talking out of my backside and feeding you rubbish.

You have no rights until you learn your rights. I want you to own the process.

Research the laws.

Start reading up on the laws around securitization. Interview a number of attorneys in town to see if there are any that would be willing to work with you and support you in this matter.

SUING YOUR LENDER

Oftentimes, challenging your lender to call them on their bluff will invariably lead to litigation. For most people, the idea of suing a big corporation is enough to make them vomit. Most would rather eat maggots than to show up in a courtroom. Before you freak out, take a deep breath. It's not as bad as you think.

Most of us fear the courtroom because of our mental association with courts. We tend to think people only need to show up in court because they are criminals or they are being sued. It sucks being on the receiving end of a civil action.

The tables turn when you are the one doing the suing. It is the other side (the bank) that will be squirming. However, you can't just go about suing the bank for no reason. Courts have rules.

If you are going to accuse someone of something, you better have proof. That's it in a nutshell. In other words, the Plaintiff (the person doing the suing) has the burden of proof.

The second rule of court is that evidence is everything. Allegations are cheap. Anyone can accuse anybody of anything. But imagine if I had a picture of a guy holding a gun, pointing at a teller with a bag of money in his hands, plus 10 other people at the scene testifying to the fact. This is something that is convincing enough to get the person convicted.

Another thing you need to know about the court system is, <u>judges do not know the law</u>.

"WHAT?!"

That's insane.

No it's not. There are literally millions of laws out there. Criminal law, family law, contract law, intellectual property law and so on. There is no way a judge could know every law that has ever been written. It is the responsibility of the litigants to bring the law before a judge so he/she can make a ruling based on evidence and law.

So, if you were to come to court showing the judge where your lender is breaking the law by bringing the appropriate laws before the court, would you feel a little better about going to court?

If you were then able to come to court with 10 reams of paper full of evidence showing where the bank lied, cheated and stole money, and you were backed up by an expert witness who used to be an ex-banker, would you feel a little better?

Would the bank feel a little squirmy?

See the difference? You just need to learn to build your case.

Imagine if you have done all your research, built your arguments, gathered a bunch of evidence about the fraud and presented this argument to a lawyer. Do you think it is more likely she will be on your side rather than tell you to take a hike? I would hope so.

The problem is, most people think the bank is the Lender and that they do have the right to foreclose. Now we know better.

The key in successfully defending against foreclosure is building and gathering your evidence.

COMMUNICATING WITH YOUR LENDER

Under the Truth in Lending Act, you are entitled to demand full disclosure from your lender.

Before jumping off the deep end, the best place to start is to write your lender to discover who they are. That might sound strange...but they are not who you think they are. You will often discover that they are, in fact, not a lender at all, but they are <u>a servicer pretending to be your lender</u>.

Try writing to your lender and ask them the following, pointblank:

> "Under the Truth in Lending Act, I have a right to know who the true party of interest in this transaction is. Please stipulate whether you are the holder in due course for my promissory note. If you are not the holder, then you admit to being the servicer of this obligation. I demand that you tell me who the holder in due course is.

Please also stipulate for the record whether or not my loan has been securitized, and if so, what the name of the REMIC/Trust my loan is bundled with."

This will give you a lot of surprising information and will help you towards getting proof of their fraud.

You might have to write two or even three letters before you get a valid response.

Many times, banks will not want to reveal their fraud. They will likely respond with a standard form letter created by a no name, minimum wage employee to the effect of:

"Your request is denied. There is no law that requires us to produce the note. Your request is frivolous. We will continue to enforce the obligation."

These letters are not signed. There is no name on the response.

You might have to copy your letter to the FTC as well as the Comptroller to the Currency (the body that governs banking in the US).

It is absolutely insulting.

However, it is imperative you document and have proof that you sent these letters as they can be used as evidence in a court of law. It is often a good idea to have a "silence through acquiescence clause" in your letter.

For example, "If you do not respond with an answer within 30 days, then you admit that this loan has been securitized and that you are merely a servicer of the obligation and not a real party of interest."

To help you get started, **I have included a sample letter on our website at http://www.consumerdefenseprograms.com** for you to use to initiate your pre-litigation discovery with your lender. Look under the Resources tab.

GETTING A MORTGAGE SCENE INVESTIGATION (SECURITIZATION AUDIT)

You've heard of CSI (Crime Scene Investigation)? Well, you should know about a new type of investigation called a MSI (Mortgage Scene Investigation).

One of the things banks hate most is a MSI, as it blatantly exposes their fraud. If banks hate it, then we love it.

Just like in a CSI where the investigator extract fingerprints, DNA and other incriminating evidence, a MSI auditor extracts incriminating evidence for your mortgage.

A MSI securitization audit is an audit done by a third party researcher who scours through EDGAR (the SEC's database for all public placements) looking for your loan. This is tedious and grueling work, as they have to literally find a needle in a haystack of a few thousand loans.

What an auditor would provide you at the end of a MSI securitization audit is a document and an affidavit that is admissible in court as evidence.

The document will show which REMIC your loan has been securitized to. Since this information is publicly available through the SEC, the affidavit is a simple statement of fact (given with firsthand knowledge) that backs up the fact that the loan has, in fact, been securitized.

As you recall, as a Plaintiff, we have the burden of proof. This is the Holy Grail of proof that is needed to prove that the bank is committing fraud.

Sadly, getting a good and reliable securitization audit can be tricky. Some companies charge as much as $4000 for one because they know the power and value of what it can do for a case.

Often times, there are outfits who supposedly offer these "securitization audits" which are utterly worthless. You have to be very cautious not to be ripped off.

Forensic vs. MSI Securitization Audits

What is the difference?

A forensic examination or audit will audit your loan documents to make sure your lender followed the law under TILA (Truth In Lending Act) and RESPA (Real Estate Settlement Procedures Act).

Some people have used the Forensic audit to stop a foreclosure claiming the lender did not do the right thing. Or did not give them appropriate disclosures, or notices of their rights, for example, the rights of rescission.

The other thing you want to look out for is the person who will be testifying for your MSI. That person will be called upon as an expert witness. Opposing Counsel will want to "destroy his reputation as an expert witness" to disqualify his information to be inadmissible in court. Having someone with experience is crucial in order to withstand this level of scrutiny.

With a good MSI audit, it's pretty much like that picture of a guy holding a gun at the bank. If your bank is caught with that smoking gun, it's a bad day to be a banker.

If you are interested in **getting an affordable MSI securitization audit,** come to http://www.consumerdefenseprograms.com. I have searched far and wide for the best and most cost-effective auditors in the country.

LEARNING THE RULES OF COURT

If you are considering taking action to defend your home, then it will be imperative that you learn how courts work. I found a fantastic resource called *Jurisdictionary by Dr. Frederic Gray.* He is an attorney who has a lot of experience with litigation cases.

As Dr. Gray points out, "Going to court is like going into a knife fight. Don't go in it with a potato peeler. Bring the biggest and baddest hatchet you can find."

<u>Don't you dare try to go to court and "wing it."</u> Go in prepared. This is your house we're talking about.

Most of us are not trained nor versed in the workings of the court. We do not have any experience in the courtroom. If you are going to take on your lender to defend your home, we recommend you learn how to fight to win.

For more information about *Jurisdictionary*, visit: www.consumerdefenseprograms.com.

HOW TO DEAL WITH LAWYERS

For the record, I think the legal profession is one of the noblest in existence and they have the potential to do the most good for the people. I have the highest respect for good lawyers who fight for the rights of the people.

Many people have asked me for recommendations of good lawyers who know foreclosure defense. Sadly, lawyers who know this stuff are few and far between.

Unfortunately, most of the time, lawyers are arrogant and deceptive. They call people without a law degree *laymen*. The idea that a layman knows something they don't know is beyond the comprehension of most lawyers.

Most lawyers (and sadly, judges, too) buy into the whole bank scam. "You borrowed the money. You enjoyed the house. You can't pay. The bank is foreclosing. What's the problem here? You're just trying to get out of the debt. This is another one of those internet scams." If they don't say as much, then their body language says it all.

I saw one situation where a person had all the evidence, and prepared a pleading. They presented it to a lawyer. The lawyer told him that he needed to put up $2000 before he would even read the documents. Two weeks later, after taking the person's money, the lawyer came back and told him, "This is crap. If you want me to handle this, I will need a $5000 retainer (and that's only to get started)." I was informed that he wanted $25,000!

I see this time and time again.

That is not to say that there aren't any good lawyers. Sadly, they are the exception rather than the rule.

Before engaging the services of a lawyer, I recommend that you buy and study up on the rules of court (buy *Jurisdictionary*). Even though your case might be handled by a lawyer, it is imperative you know what the lawyer is doing (or not doing, for that matter).

I also recommend that you do as much of the homework as possible to build your case. Gather the evidence. Do the Mortgage Scene Investigation (MSI) securitization audit. Take your first crack at building your own pleading. Do a Google search on the Internet. Look for a template for a *quiet title action* or *wrongful foreclosure*. Start reading up on what others have done.

This will save you money and several headaches... and increase your chances of success.

It is hard enough dealing with the stress of losing your home and the prospect of fighting the bank. You don't need to fight your own counsel. Interview any lawyer you intend to work with. See if they have done any previous litigation or know about commercial law. Most importantly, see if the person is someone who is open minded and someone you can trust. Use your gut. If you don't like the guy, then I don't care how good he is—run.

When working with a lawyer, you should be a thorn in his side (in a good way). Don't just leave it to him. You should always be on top of your lawyer. Make sure he is accountable for how many hours he spends on your case. If you are going to pay someone $250/hour, you have the right to know what he is working on and when. A common tactic lawyers use is to have paralegals do their work for them. They would charge you their lawyer's rate and have the paralegal do the work. Make sure you get clear distinctions between these rates.

My main concern with lawyers is that they see their clients not as people suffering from bank fraud, but as buckets of money. You pay them a retainer. You are hard on your luck. You barely have a roof over your head, and you need help. Yet these people see a retainer as an invitation to rip you off. Their objective is to do anything and everything they can to spend that retainer as quickly as possible and hit you up for more. If you run out of money, their response is "Sorry. Tough luck." It seems like once these people get their Bar certificate, they made a deal with the Devil and traded their humanity and soul away. Some people have taken to calling them "Bar flies."

Here's why you may not want the most experienced and sharpest one you can find. They are often in high demand, they don't need the work, and they don't have the time to properly prepare and research your case. Instead, it might be better to find a friendly attorney and bring him a case with solid arguments, solid evidence and solid laws to back it up. All he has to do is to massage it. All you have to do is to make sure he IS actually REPRESENTING (talking on your behalf, using your arguments) you.

One way to weed out crappy lawyers is to give them this book and ask them to read it. We have written this book with the purpose of not only exposing the fraud, but also showing lawyers how to argue the case. A good lawyer can take what we have presented here and do their own research to support the arguments presented here. If they are not willing to read it or demand that you pay them for THEIR EDUCATION, then they might not be someone you want to work with.

One key point you want to enlighten potential lawyers you intend to work with is that this is a major growth area of law. If they learn the arguments of foreclosure defense, they will likely have a lot more business and a huge competitive advantage over other lawyers in town.

Again, there are likely good lawyers out there. Unfortunately, many of them are often booked up and are hard to find.

The advantage of a good lawyer is that they can prepare your arguments, make sure they are legally sufficient and be able to represent you in court. Since he should have experience in the courtroom, he would know what to say and do.

As boring and as weird as it may sound, learn to love the law. It is there for you.

If you are looking for a lawyer or know of a good one you can refer other members to, please come to our site and check our referrals under the Resources tab: http://www.consumerdefenseprograms.com.

DO IT YOURSELF

If you can't afford a lawyer or can't find a good one to work with, the next option is to do it yourself. This is known as pro se (or pro per in California).

More and more homeowners are choosing to do it on their own. Frankly, this information is so exotic and so new that few people can rely on lawyers to support them.

Let's be clear. This is not easy. This could be one of the most demanding things you have ever been asked to do in your life.

Don't Do This.

Seriously, this is not a standard disclaimer. **Don't do this.** The litigation process is not for the weak of heart.

It is better that you find other solutions than to litigate against your lender half cocked. It's like a fly hitting a windshield. It is not pretty if you don't know what you are doing.

That said, your home is everything. Without it, you are lost. You are ungrounded and uprooted. Your family is unsettled.

Now that you know about the fraud, you have to decide whether you are willing to fight for your rights. However, if you do decide to do this, you will have to commit to doing it to the very end.

As Yoda says "Do, or do not. There is no try."

I have put together a coaching membership program to help homeowners with resources so they can do this on their own.

Our membership program allows you to connect with other homeowners so that you can support each other, share and collaborate on ideas. As a benefit of the membership program, you will also receive sample documents you can use to challenge your lender and fight for your rights. Other benefits include:

- **Access to sample responses**. Once a lender responds, I have samples used by others in our program that you can use to craft your own responses.

- **Legal Resources**. I will show you where to go to look for local laws as it applies to you and where you can find people to help prepare documents who understand this process and more.

- **Group Conference Calls** where you can ask and collaborate with members on a weekly basis.

- **Guest speakers**. We bring experts from around the country to talk about mortgage defense successes to give you ideas to help you with your situation.

- **Access to our Archives**. We have over 40 hours of archive content that will be available exclusively to members of our community.

- **Drip Delivered Content.** Instead of dumping you with hours and hours of content, we give you day by day automated content delivery so that you are never lost. Our automated system will tell you when to send out letters, when to order a MSI securitization audit, when to go to the county recorder's office for research, and more.

Let's be clear. This is a membership to a homeowner's support club, and is not a substitute for good competent legal advice. You should seek competent legal counsel where possible. (Sorry, I am required to tell you this. The Bar Association has a monopoly on the legal franchise.) This is an automated coaching system. No personal coaching is included (I just don't have the time to).

For more information about our foreclosure defense membership program, come to: http://www.consumerdefenseprograms.com/coaching-program/intro/. It is more affordable than you think.

HELP, MY HOUSE IS UP FOR SALE NEXT WEEK!

If you find yourself in a situation where you are about to lose your home, you have two options legally.

One is to file a civil action against your lender followed by a motion for a Temporary Restraining Order (TRO) and Injunctive Relief. The other is to file for bankruptcy protection with an automatic stay.

Firstly, in order for a TRO and/or an Injunctive Relief to be granted, the petitioner has to show a strong likelihood of success. This means that as a Plaintiff, you will need to bring compelling evidence to convince the judge that you deserve a stay of the sale. It is your job to bring significant controversy that brings doubt as to who the real party of interest is in the foreclosure action.

Obviously, having a MSI securitization audit would be hugely beneficial as well as a pleading/complaint that argues the points and authority that the lender is not the real party of interest. However, this takes time. Time you might not have.

Crafting a pleading takes time and requires great care. It is not something that can be rushed. You should consult your lawyer as to the proper method and process for this.

If you are a member of our <u>foreclosure defense membership program</u>, I have included sample TROs, Injunctive Reliefs as well as sample pleadings that others have used. It is then up to you to customize the arguments as it applies to your own situation. Be warned. You do so at your own risk. These sample documents do not come with any assurances whatsoever.

Sadly, **TROs are RARELY granted**. The Plaintiff has to bring an **overwhelming** amount of evidence to cast significant doubt to the judge for one to be granted.

THE BANKRUPTCY AUTOMATIC STAY METHOD

To buy time, some homeowners declare bankruptcy. When you declare bankruptcy, you receive an automatic stay from all creditors, including the lender.

Many homeowners feel this is the best and most assured way to stop the sale from happening.

Be warned. Bankruptcy is not for the weak hearted. Do not enter bankruptcy lightly.

You will need to declare all your assets, income and financial details. It is like having a permanent anal probe of your financial details. It is not pleasant.

<u>Never ever lie, especially in bankruptcy court. You will go to jail.</u> As great as the temptation to hide the precious little money you have from your creditors is, don't do it.

The other down side of bankruptcy is that it is a mark in your public credit score. But frankly, having a bankruptcy or a foreclosure these days is not as big a deal as it once was. Almost half the country has been through it. It's like being a leper in a leper colony. It's not as big a deal anymore.

The fact is, however, for most homeowners **this might be the only way to keep their house from the auction block** while they buy time to build their case for their foreclosure defense.

The other thing about bankruptcy is that in my experience, I have found that most of the wins come from the bankruptcy courts. The thing about bankruptcy is that it has the nice Rule 3001(d).

It requires the lender to provide proof of claim.

This means that the table is suddenly turned. It is now the lender who has to come up with the proof of claim. And if you know how their fraud is being perpetrated, then you know how to object and deflect their deception.

> **Federal Rules of Bankruptcy 3001 (d) Evidence of perfection of security interest.**
>
> *If a security interest in property of the debtor is claimed, the proof of claim shall be accompanied **by evidence that the security interest has been perfected**.*

What many people do after they file for bankruptcy is to file an *adversary proceeding*. As a debtor, this is absolutely free. An adversary proceeding is like a normal civil action, but done under bankruptcy court, and under bankruptcy rules. It allows the debtor to challenge the bank to provide proof of standing.

The other thing many home-owners do is file their house as an unsecured debt. This will then prompt the lender to complain. But in doing so, they are then required to provide proof of claim, which they often are unable to. It is important

> Please note, **you cannot file an adversary proceeding under Chapter 7.** This is very important to remember.

to compel your Trustee (if you are going through Chapter 7) to force the lender to follow Bankruptcy Rule 3001(d).

Navigating the bankruptcy process is not for the weak hearted. Even for someone who has a lot of experience in legal procedures. I **highly** (seriously, HIGHLY) **recommend** that you get competent help. Look, I am here to save you money. If I HIGHLY recommend something, I mean it. Some things you can cut corners with, but <u>bankruptcy is something I don't recommend that you do on your own</u>. I have a M.B.A. Trust me when I tell you that I tried to do it myself. It was a disaster. I wished I had professional help.

Normally, hiring a law firm to handle your bankruptcy costs from $2000 to $4000 for Chapter 13. I found a company (not related to us) that specializes in preparing bankruptcy documents who can do it for less than $1000.

If you are interested in this service, come to www.consumerdefenseprograms.com. It is listed under Resources.

In the next chapter, I go into the practical matter of "now I know that there is fraud going on with my house, what can I do about it?"

CHAPTER 8:
PRACTICAL MATTERS

In this chapter, I go through specific practical things you can do right away to challenge your lender.

At its heart, there are four classes of people that are affected by foreclosures.

1. Someone who is about to lose his or her home in a **Non-Judicial State** (California, Nevada, Arizona, Oregon, Washington, etc)

2. Someone who is about to lose his or her home in a **Judicial State** (New York, New Jersey, Ohio, Florida, etc)

3. Someone who has already **lost his or her home**

4. Someone who is hanging by their teeth, who is upside down or can no longer pay their mortgage trying to get a **loan modification or someone in good standing.**

Each class of person has different options and procedures available to them. This chapter will outline in brief some of these options. Of course, this is just a book and is no substitute for competent legal advice, so please consult counsel before doing anything that could affect your home.

NON-JUDICIAL STATE HOMEOWNERS

Most Western States of the US are Non-Judicial States. In these States, foreclosures are governed by State Civil Code.

These homeowners have it the toughest. Being in a judicial state, Lenders need not prove anything. They can simply notify the homeowner of the default, then after a certain number of days as defined under State Civil Code, the property then proceeds to a Trustee sale at a public auction.

The only option available to you if you are a non-Judicial State resident is for you to file a civil action against your lender to compel them to provide proof of claim, and therefore standing.

The other option is to declare bankruptcy (also known as BK). In bankruptcy, generally speaking, you have two options, Chapter 7 (no asset BK) or a Chapter 13 (asset BK). What some homeowners do is to declare Chapter 7 and list their property as an unsecured asset and wait for the lender to object. This then puts the burden of proof on the lender. If your loan was closed with Lender A and is being foreclosed on by Lender B or C....there must be (by law) a valid chain of assignment to show that Lender C is the real and beneficial party of interest. As I discussed, because of the problem of securitization, this is never done. This creates a real problem for the Lender (who is frankly doing this in fraud anyway).

For those with a lot of assets (such as equity in their homes), they can do a Chapter 13. Under a Chapter 13 bankruptcy, you can file an Adversary Proceeding where you sue your lender to compel them to produce valid proof of claim. The beauty with Bankruptcy Court is that you have the law on your side. Rule 3001(d) of the Federal Code of Bankruptcy requires that your lender provide evidence of "perfected title".

If you choose to file a civil action against your lender, you better have proof as I discussed earlier. The best proof you can bring is a MSI securitization audit to prove that your loan has been securitized. Then, work with your lawyer to build an argument around the points outlined in this book. Unfortunately, this will set you back at the minimum $5000, and more likely closer to $10,000 to $25,000.

Another option you could do is to do a "quick reconveyance method" as discussed in Chapter 4. This can be very effective in stopping your servicer's ability to foreclose because it closes out the Deed of Trust/Mortgage. This method is only applicable when you have clear evidence of movement or securitization. You can find out more about this method on our website under the Products tab.

Alternatively, if you cannot afford a lawyer, you could try to do this yourself. Great places to start are **LivingLies.com** and **stopforeclosurefraud.com**. These are blogs with lots of articles, sample pleadings and lots of other resources and I used during my research.

Another option is to join our foreclosure defense membership program. I realized that there are SO MANY homeowners needing help. That is why

I developed a coaching membership program with specific information and resources to help homeowners with their foreclosure defense. Our membership program has sample pleadings, sample responses, forms and procedures others have used in their foreclosure defense. You will also able to network with other homeowners local to you...meet with them to have coffee, and support each other. For more information about this program, come to our website at: http://www.consumerdefenseprograms.com

A good place to start if you are in a non-Judicial State is to start writing to your lender to demand that they produce valid proof of claim. You can find a couple of sample letters on our site. This will be a good place to get started.

JUDICIAL STATE HOMEOWNERS

In a Judicial State, your lender has to sue you to get a judgment before they can foreclose on your house. As I discussed earlier, the burden of proof is on the plaintiff. This means that if you are in a Judicial State, you have the advantage of requiring the lender to produce proof of claim.

The problem in most cases is that homeowners in Judicial States do not know the nature of foreclosure fraud. They either don't show up or if they show up, don't know how to argue their points and thus end up losing their homes anyway.

The other problem in Judicial States is that because there are so many cases, judges end up forgoing their Oath of Office to the people they serve. Instead of dispensing justice fairly to all, they rubber-stamp judgments without a second glance. This is not fair to the homeowners, but if homeowners don't know their rights, nor know how to argue their points, then sadly, there's little justice for them. As they say, you have no rights unless you know what those rights are.

So, the best thing to do if you are a resident of a Judicial State then is to arm yourself with education. Learn the nature of loan fraud. Learn the procedure of rules of court, and how to defend yourself in answering a summons and complaint.

You should know by now that your best course of action is to push the Federal Rules of Civil Procedure 17, "an action has to be taken in the name of a real party of interest"...in other words, you are to challenge your lender's Standing and their right to foreclose. If they are not a real and beneficial party of interest, then they do not have the right to foreclose. In allowing them to proceed with their foreclosure without Standing amounts to nothing more than theft and extortion. Both of which are illegal.

Other homeowners in Judicial States choose to take a more proactive approach. Instead of waiting to be sued by their lender, they do a securitization audit, gather evidence of loan securitization, and then sue their lender to get a Quiet Title Action to remove the Mortgage from their property since no one can come forth to produce valid proof of claim.

For members of our foreclosure defense membership program, I have sample templates that homeowners can use to take matters into their own hands.

Homeowners Who Have Lost Their Homes

For those homeowners who have already lost their homes, there are two situations. There are those who have lost their homes due to a sale but are still staying in their homes, and there are those who have been forced to move out.

Many lawyers and people in the media are advising homeowners who have lost their homes but are still living in them to **stay in their homes**. It could take months sometimes for the lender to come around to actually force the homeowner out.

Typically, in order for a lender to force a homeowner to move out, they will need to file for an "unlawful detainer". This takes a while to be granted, and this gives the homeowner additional time. Staying another month or three at home means another few more months they do not have to pay rent elsewhere.

Another technique homeowners do is to challenge the lender's standing to foreclose even after the fact to fight the unlawful detainer. This is something you will likely need to consult with an attorney for more information.

The Wrongful Foreclosure Action

Homeowners who have already lost their homes but believe their loans have been securitized might want to see if they can do a Wrongful Foreclosure civil action against their "pretender lenders".

Here are some hints that your loans have been securitized are:

- There is a company called MERS (Mortgage Electronic Registration Systems) involved in the Notice of Substitution of Trustee, or on the original Deed of Trust/Mortgage (this is usually on the first 2 pages of your documents).
- Your loan is with one of the following institutions: GMAC, Countrywide Home Loans, Bank of America, Wells Fargo, or Chase.
- You closed with a small no name bank, and you are now being serviced by a more well known institution like the ones named above.

If you can gather sufficient evidence that your loan has been securitized, then you might be able to build a case using the arguments presented in this book to bring a civil action against your lender for a wrongful foreclosure and/or fraud. Essentially, you are accusing your lender of committing fraud in that they did not have Standing to foreclose on your property.

In a civil action in which you have suffered damages as a result of something the other party have done against you, **typically you are entitled to three times the damages(three times the value of your loan).** This is typically called "punitive damages". It means it is damages other than documented real financial/physical harm. This includes stress, torment, humiliation, etc. Again, this is something you should bring up with your attorney.

Before talking to an attorney (and wasting a lot of money), you ought to make sure you have a case. In court, the truth is irrelevant. Evidence is everything. It's a sad fact of the system. It is your job to bring a strong case with plenty of strong evidence of wrong doing before you can even begin accusing your lender of any wrong doing.

The best way to start is to get a Mortgage Scene Investigation (MSI) securitization audit. Look in the "What are my Options" chapter for more information about getting a MSI audit.

Next, you would want to do more research about the problems of securitizations and build your case and arguments. Good places to start include:

- ConsumerDefensePrograms.com
- LivingLies.com
- stopForeclosureFraud.com
- 4closureFraud.com
- MyPrivateAudio.com

Remember, you have no rights unless you know what your rights are. Your "lender" is not about to volunteer information that will allow you to burn them with. It's your job to dig these up.

Getting a Contingency Lawyer

Look, most of us have our backs against the wall. We are barely surviving. We don't have money, and we don't have the time to study up on the law to take on the bank by ourselves. And, hiring a lawyer on a "maybe" is not money necessarily well spent.

Getting a contingency lawyer might be a really good option for many people.

However, there is no shortage of opportunities for Contingency lawyers. These lawyers get their choice as to what cases they want to take. It is your job to bring them a case that is worth a lot of money, delivered on a silver plate. Make it a "no brainer" for these lawyers to want to work with you. The best way to do this is to have everything prepared, ready to go. This means that you have a MSI securitization audit, a basic pleading and argument already in place, any applicable laws that can be used in support of your case.

Be warned. A contingency lawyer will likely eat up a large percentage of your settlement. I have heard of cases where they eat up as much as 70% of your settlement. That said, there is a proverb I want to share with you.

100% of nothing is still nothing.

A 20% to 40% of a multi-million dollar settlement is still a good deal, especially you didn't know you had a case in the first place.

But, I would advise that you do your homework and bring your case on a silver platter.

Honestly, the most dangerous position for a banker is a determined homeowner who has already lost their home. It's like having a photo of a guy holding a gun, pointing at a teller with a bag of cash under his arms. All the evidence is already there. It just takes determination to assemble the evidence forensically to build a case.

For help with a post foreclosure coaching, I have another membership program that supports homeowners through the process with sample pleadings and other resources at http://www.consumerdefenseprograms.com.

LOAN MODIFICATION APPLICANTS

For those of you in the middle of a loan modification, chances are good that you will not be given a loan modification. As I outlined earlier in this book, loan modifications are a scam. Your lender does not own the note. Frankly, there is no real incentive for them to grant you a loan modification. **It is your job to push the issue and make it in your lender's best interest to deal with you fairly before you bring them to court.**

How do you do this?

Imagine if we were playing a three shell game. Let's say I am a scammer and I have very swift hands. Somehow, I was able to swipe the ball (and there are no balls in play at all). The typical rule of the game is for you to point to where the ball is, I will then lift that cup. If the ball is under the cup you pointed, then you win. If not, I win. Now, imagine if you point at the two OTHER

CUPS...forcing me to lift those two cups. By a process of elimination and deduction, the ball therefore MUST BE UNDER THE REMAINDER CUP. Because we both know the scam, you are going to give me an out. You are going to give me a wink (as to say, I know your scam), and I will read the hint and will then say "congratulations, you won. Now go away kid, you are hurting my business." ie. I know that you know that there is no ball, but in order to maintain the illusion, I am forced to admit that the ball must be under the last cup.

What I am saying is, you will basically build all the arguments to prove to your lender that you know their fraud. You bring all the evidence to prove that they don't own the note. You build your pleading as if you are going to sue them, and send them a letter informing of your intention to file suite. You then tell your lender that to save the pain of litigation, you propose that they deal fairly with you for a fair loan modification and principle reduction.

You see, if you present them an offer they cannot refuse, then you are coming into the negotiation from a position of power.

You always want to negotiate from a position of power, not from a position of weakness. Most homeowners approach loan modifications from a position of desperation. As in "please. I am begging you. I desperately need you to give me a loan modification before I go into foreclosure."

I am just showing you a different approach. This process works because in one instance, one of my friends sued the CEO of Bank of America. It was AMAZING how fast the offer for a loan modification came in because the CEO personally pushed for the loan modification to be approved no matter what.

Good luck. I know these are desperate times. But we need to be persistent. Don't be a sheeple. Wake up. Take proactive action.

I'M NOT IN DEFAULT YET

Let's be clear. In no way do I advocate that you stop making payments and deliberately go into default now that you have discovered this fraud.

If fact, if you are in good standing, your chances of fighting foreclosure fraud is even greater because of the following:

1) In a Non-Judicial State, once you are in default, the State Civil Code takes over and your rights are greatly diminished. The "lender" does not need to prove anything and if you fight them in court, they will tell you (and the judge) so. And it's true.

2) The real and beneficial parties of interest are the individual shareholders of the REMIC. Your debt has not been passed around in the secondary market. This makes the allegations very specific in your Quiet Title Action and the other side has very little place to hide.

If you are in good standing, the best place to start is to start writing your "lender" (aka servicer) and demand to know full disclosure of the real parties involved. Use the sample letters on the website at http://www.consumerdefenseprograms.com. Have your "lender" disclose whether your loan has been securitized and to which REMIC.

Then get a MSI securitization audit (of if you can figure out how to do one on your own through looking at the SEC database).

Next, start a litigation process against your "lender" under a Quiet Title Action. You are advised to best get a lawyer to work with you in this process.

If you choose to do it on your own, you might want to consider joining our foreclosure defense membership program where I provide you with sample Quiet Title Action pleadings others have used in the past as well as other support resources to help you fight foreclosure fraud.

START LOCAL GROUPS

Look, this problem affects everyone. When sections of houses are foreclosed on, it affects local communities. We have situations where there are literally hundreds of houses sitting empty, while thousands of families live in tent cities around the country.

All the while our banker friends are getting millions of dollars in bonuses from OUR TAXPAYER MONEY.

I encourage you to get together with people in your community to talk about this. Raise each other's awareness.

We are in the middle of a global economic depression. Everyone is suffering. And it isn't getting better. One of the ways we can change it around is by claiming our homes possibly free and clear (or otherwise, get a fair loan modification that we can actually afford). Imagine if instead of paying $2000 a month on your mortgage, you can use that towards a new car, or towards your children's education. Start injecting money back into the economy to create real local jobs again.

Together, we can each make a difference. But you have to get off the couch and take action.

TAKING ON THE FIGHT

If what I have written speaks to you and have inspired you to take action then I have done my job. However, that said, I am advising you to **slow down**.

Don't Do This.

As cruel as it sounds, I am again advising you against doing this process as I have outlined. It is a lot of work and frankly is very painful. **This process is not easy.** You will not be able to sleep. Every time the phone rings, you feel like vomiting because you think it might be your lender or their lawyer calling you. Every time you receive a letter from the lender or their lawyer, you feel like someone has punched you in the guts.

To file a civil action against your lender is not something for the weak of heart.

However, if you do decide to do something about it, then welcome to the movement. You should commit to doing it all the way.

Never approach a lion's den and halfway during the fight drop your shield and run. You will be eaten. The same goes to this process. If you decide to do this process, then you should commit to finishing it. As they say, "never start a fight you are not willing to finish".

This is perhaps the hardest thing you will have to do in your lifetime. It is the classic epic battle of life and death. David vs. Goliath. This is the fight to save your family. It is worth fighting for. It means that your children will have a roof over their heads instead of living in a tent city.

It is for this reason we created our membership program so homeowners can support each other. We've made it affordable so everyone can join...but like any organization, it takes money to maintain. We have staff to feed, and servers to maintain. Your support means we can continue to do this research and support our members.

For more information, come to our site at http://www.consumerdefenseprograms.com.

PLEASE SPREAD THE NEWS

Our mission is to awaken people to the problem of foreclosure fraud. If you know someone in the press, send a copy of this book to them.

Pass this on to someone. Make a difference. Give this book to someone who can benefit from the information contained in this book. We are all connected. What happens to one of us affects us all.

If you are on Facebook, please tell your friends about it. Post a link to our site.

I hope you will join us.

Vince Khan

and

Your Friends at Consumer Defense Programs.

APPENDIX

The following are supporting documents from various different sources that expose bank fraud.

APPENDIX A: CFR TITLE 12: BANKS AND BANKING

PART 226—TRUTH IN LENDING (REGULATION Z)

§ 226.39 Mortgage transfer disclosures.

Link to an amendment published at 75 FR 58501, Sept. 24, 2010.

(a) *Scope.* The disclosure requirements of this section apply to any covered person except as otherwise provided in this section. For purposes of this section:

(1) A *"covered person"* means any person, as defined in §226.2(a)(22), that becomes the owner of an existing mortgage loan by acquiring legal title to the debt obligation, whether through a purchase, assignment, or other transfer, and who acquires more than one mortgage loan in any twelve-month period. **For purposes of this section, a servicer of a mortgage loan shall not be treated as the owner of the obligation** if the servicer holds title to the loan or it is assigned to the servicer solely for the administrative convenience of the servicer in servicing the obligation.

(2) A *"mortgage loan"* means any consumer credit transaction that is secured by the principal dwelling of a consumer.

(b) *Disclosure required.* Except as provided in paragraph (c) of this section, any person that becomes a covered person as defined in this section shall mail or deliver the disclosures required by this section to the consumer on or before the 30th calendar day following the acquisition date. If there is more than one covered person, only one disclosure shall be given and the covered persons shall agree among themselves which covered person shall comply with the requirements that this section imposes on any or all of them.

(1) *Acquisition date.* For purposes of this section, the date that the covered person acquired the mortgage loan shall be the date of acquisition recognized in the books and records of the acquiring party.

(2) *Multiple consumers.* If there is more than one consumer liable on the obligation, a covered person may mail or deliver the disclosures to any consumer who is primarily liable.

(c) *Exceptions.* Notwithstanding paragraph (b) of this section, a covered person is not subject to the requirements of this section with respect to a particular mortgage loan if:

(1) The covered person sells or otherwise transfers or assigns legal title to the mortgage loan on or before the 30th calendar day following the date that the covered person acquired the mortgage loan; or

(2) The mortgage loan is transferred to the covered person in connection with a repurchase agreement and the transferor that is obligated to

repurchase the loan continues to recognize the loan as an asset on its own books and records. However, if the transferor does not repurchase the mortgage loan, the acquiring party must make the disclosures required by §226.39 within 30 days after the date that the transaction is recognized as an acquisition in its books and records.

(d) *Content of required disclosures.* The disclosures required by this section shall identify the loan that was acquired or transferred and state the following:

(1) The identity, address, and telephone number of the covered person who owns the mortgage loan. If there is more than one covered person, the information required by this paragraph shall be provided for each of them.

(2) The acquisition date recognized by the covered person.

(3) How to reach an agent or party having authority to act on behalf of the covered person (or persons), which shall identify a person (or persons) authorized to receive legal notices on behalf of the covered person and resolve issues concerning the consumer's payments on the loan. However, no information is required to be provided under this paragraph if the consumer can use the information provided under paragraph (d)(1) of this section for these purposes. If multiple persons are identified under this paragraph, the disclosure shall provide contact information for each and indicate the extent to which the authority of each agent

differs. For purposes of this paragraph (d)(3), it is sufficient if the covered person provides only a telephone number provided that the consumer can use the telephone number to obtain the address for the agent or other person identified.

(4) The location where transfer of ownership of the debt to the covered person is recorded. However, if the transfer of ownership has not been recorded in public records at the time the disclosure is provided, the covered person complies with this paragraph by stating this fact.

(e) *Optional disclosures.* In addition to the information required to be disclosed under paragraph (d) of this section, a covered person may, at its option, provide any other information regarding the transaction.

APPENDIX B: FAIR DEBT COLLECTIONS PRACTICES ACT - DEBT VALIDATION LETTER

USC Title 15 § 1692g. Here is the Fair Debt Collections Practices Act in regards to validation of debts.

§ 809. VALIDATION OF DEBTS

(a) Within five days after the initial communication with a consumer in connection with the collection of any debt, a debt collector shall, unless the following information is contained in the initial communication or the consumer has paid the debt, send the consumer a written notice containing—

(1) the amount of the debt;

(2) the name of the creditor to whom the debt is owed;

(3) a statement that unless the consumer, within thirty days after receipt of the notice, disputes the validity of the debt, or any portion thereof, the debt will be assumed to be valid by the debt collector;

(4) a statement that if the consumer notifies the debt collector in writing within the thirty-day period that the debt, or any portion thereof, is disputed, the debt collector will obtain verification of the debt or a copy of a judgment against the consumer and a copy of such verification or judgment will be mailed to the consumer by the debt collector; and

(5) a statement that, upon the consumer's written request within the thirty-day period, the

debt collector will provide the consumer with the name and address of the original creditor, if different from the current creditor.

(b) If the consumer notifies the debt collector in writing within the thirty-day period described in subsection (a) that the debt, or any portion thereof, is disputed, or that the consumer requests the name and address of the original creditor, the debt collector shall cease collection of the debt, or any disputed portion thereof, until the debt collector obtains verification of the debt or any copy of a judgment, or the name and address of the original creditor, and a copy of such verification or judgment, or name and address of the original creditor, is mailed to the consumer by the debt collector. Collection activities and communications that do not otherwise violate this title may continue during the 30-day period referred to in subsection (a) unless the consumer has notified the debt collector in writing that the debt, or any portion of the debt, is disputed or that do not otherwise violate this title may continue during the 30-day period referred to in subsection (a) unless the consumer has notified the debt collector in writing that the debt, or any portion of the debt, is disputed or that the consumer requests the name and address of the original creditor. Any collection activities and communication during the 30-day period may not overshadow or be inconsistent with the disclosure of the consumer's right to dispute the debt or request the name and address of the original creditor.

(c) The failure of a consumer to dispute the validity of a debt under this section may not be construed by any court as an admission of liability by the consumer.

(d) A communication in the form of a formal pleading in a civil action shall not be treated as an initial communication for purposes of subsection (a).

(e) The sending or delivery of any form or notice which does not relate to the collection of a debt and is expressly required by the Internal Revenue Code of 1986, title V of Gramm-Leach-Bliley Act, or any provision of Federal or State law relating to notice of data security breach or privacy, or any regulation prescribed under any such provision of law, shall not be treated as an initial communication in connection with debt collection for purposes of this section

APPENDIX C: HOMEOWNER WINS: CASE LAW SUCCESSES

Patton v. Diemer, 35 Ohio St. 3d 68; 518 N.E.2d 941; 1988). A judgment rendered by a court lacking subject matter jurisdiction is void ab initio. Consequently, the authority to vacate a void judgment is not derived from Ohio R. Civ. P. 60(B), but rather constitutes an inherent power possessed by Ohio courts. I see no evidence to the contrary that this would apply to ALL courts.

.

"A party lacks standing to invoke the jurisdiction of a court unless he has, in an individual or a representative capacity, some real interest in the subject matter of the action. Lebanon Correctional Institution v. Court of **Common Pleas 35 Ohio St.2d 176 (1973)**.

.

"A party lacks standing to invoke the jurisdiction of a court unless he has, in an individual or a representative capacity, some real interest in the subject matter of an action." **Wells Fargo Bank, v. Byrd, 178 Ohio App.3d 285, 2008-Ohio-4603, 897 N.E.2d 722 (2008)**. It went on to hold, "If plaintiff has offered no evidence that it owned the note and mortgage when the complaint was filed, it would not be entitled to judgment as a matter of law."

.

(The following court case was unpublished and hidden from the public) **Wells Fargo, Litton Loan v. Farmer, 867 N.Y.S.2d 21 (2008)**. "Wells Fargo does not own the mortgage loan... Therefore, the... matter is dismissed with prejudice."

.

(The following court case was unpublished and hidden from the public) **Wells Fargo v. Reyes, 867 N.Y.S.2d 21 (2008).** Dismissed with prejudice, Fraud on Court & Sanctions. Wells Fargo never owned the Mortgage.

.

(The following court case was unpublished and hidden from the public) **Deutsche Bank v. Peabody, 866 N.Y.S.2d 91 (2008).** EquiFirst, when making the loan, violated Regulation Z of the Federal Truth in Lending Act 15 USC §1601 and the Fair Debt Collections Practices Act 15 USC §1692; "intentionally created fraud in the factum" and withheld from plaintiff... "vital information concerning said debt and all of the matrix involved in making the loan."

.

(The following court case was unpublished and hidden from the public) **Indymac Bank v. Boyd, 880 N.Y.S.2d 224 (2009).** To establish a prima facie case in an action to foreclose a mortgage, the plaintiff must establish the existence of the mortgage and the mortgage note. It is the law's policy to allow only an aggrieved person to bring a lawsuit . . . A want of "standing to sue," in other words, is just another way of saying that this particular plaintiff is not involved in a genuine controversy, and a simple syllogism takes us from there to a "jurisdictional" dismissal:

.

(The following court case was unpublished and hidden from the public) **Indymac Bank v. Bethley, 880 N.Y.S.2d 873 (2009).** The Court is concerned that there may be fraud on the part of plaintiff or at least malfeasance Plaintiff INDYMAC (Deutsche) and must have "standing" to bring this action.

.

(The following court case was unpublished and hidden from the public) **Deutsche Bank National Trust Co v.Torres, NY Slip Op 51471U (2009).** That "the dead cannot be sued" is a well established principle of the jurisprudence of this state plaintiff's second cause of action for declaratory relief is denied. To be entitled to a default judgment, the movant must establish, among other things, the existence of facts which give rise to viable claims against the defaulting defendants.

.

"The doctrine of ultra vires is a most powerful weapon to keep private corporations within their legitimate spheres and punish them for violations of their corporate charters, and it probably is not invoked too often..." **Zinc Carbonate Co. v. First National Bank, 103 Wis. 125, 79 NW 229 (1899).** Also see: American Express Co. v. Citizens State Bank, 181 Wis. 172, 194 NW 427 (1923).

.

(The following court case was unpublished and hidden from the public) **Wells Fargo v. Reyes, 867 N.Y.S.2d 21 (2008).** Case dismissed with prejudice, fraud on the Court and Sanctions because Wells Fargo never owned the Mortgage.

.

(The following court case was unpublished and hidden from the public) **Wells Fargo, Litton Loan v. Farmer, 867 N.Y.S.2d 21 (2008).** Wells Fargo does not own the mortgage loan. "Indeed, no more than (affidavits) is necessary to make the prima facie case." United States v. Kis, 658 F.2d, 526 (7th Cir. 1981).

.

(The following court case was unpublished and hidden from the public) **Indymac Bank v. Bethley, 880 N.Y.S.2d 873 (2009).** The Court is concerned that there may be fraud on the part of plaintiff or at least malfeasance Plaintiff INDYMAC (Deutsche) and must have "standing" to bring this action.

.

Lawyer responsible for false debt collection claim Fair Debt Collection Practices Act, 15 USCS §§ 1692-1692o,**Heintz v. Jenkins, 514 U.S. 291; 115 S. Ct. 1489, 131 L. Ed. 2d 395 (1995).** and FDCPA Title 15 U.S.C. sub section 1692.

.

In determining whether the plaintiffs come before this Court with clean hands, the primary factor to be considered is whether the plaintiffs sought to mislead or deceive the other party, not whether that party relied upon plaintiffs' misrepresentations. **Stachnik v. Winkel, 394 Mich. 375, 387; 230 N.W.2d 529, 534 (1975).**

.

"Indeed, no more than (affidavits) is necessary to make the prima facie case." **United States v.**

Kis, 658 F.2d, 526 (7th Cir. 1981). Cert Denied, 50 U.S. L.W. 2169; S. Ct. March 22, (1982).

.

"Silence can only be equated with fraud where there is a legal or moral duty to speak or when an inquiry left unanswered would be intentionally misleading." **U.S. v. Tweel, 550 F.2d 297 (1977).**

.

"If any part of the consideration for a promise be illegal, or if there are several considerations for an un-severable promise one of which is illegal, the promise, whether written or oral, is wholly void, as it is impossible to say what part or which one of the considerations induced the promise." **Menominee River Co. v. Augustus Spies L & C Co., 147 Wis. 559 at p. 572; 132 NW 1118 (1912).**

.

Federal Rule of Civil Procedure 17(a)(1) which requires that "[a]n action must be prosecuted in the name of the real party in interest." See also, In re Jacobson, 402 B.R. 359, 365-66 (Bankr. W.D. Wash. 2009); In re Hwang, 396 B.R. 757, 766-67 (Bankr. C.D. Cal. 2008).

.

Mortgage Electronic Registration Systems, Inc. v. Chong, 824 N.Y.S.2d 764 (2006). MERS did not have standing as a real party in interest under the Rules to file the motion... The declaration also failed to assert that MERS, FMC Capital LLC or Homecomings Financial, LLC held the Note.

.

Landmark National Bank v. Kesler, 289 Kan. 528, 216 P.3d 158 (2009). "Kan. Stat. Ann. § 60-260(b) allows relief from a judgment based on mistake, inadvertence, surprise, or excusable neglect; newly discovered evidence that could not have been timely discovered with due diligence; fraud or misrepresentation; a void judgment; a judgment that has been satisfied, released, discharged, or is no longer equitable; or any other reason justifying relief from the operation of the judgment. The relationship that the registry had to the bank was more akin to that of a straw man than to a party possessing all the rights given a buyer." Also In September of 2008, A California Judge ruling against MERS concluded, "There is no evidence before the court as to who is the present owner of the Note. The holder of the Note must join in the motion."

.

LaSalle Bank v. Ahearn, 875 N.Y.S.2d 595 (2009). Dismissed with prejudice. Lack of standing.

.

Novastar Mortgage, Inc v. Snyder 3:07CV480 (2008). Plaintiff has the burden of establishing its standing. It has failed to do so.

.

DLJ Capital, Inc. v. Parsons, CASE NO. 07-MA-17 (2008). A genuine issue of material fact existed as to whether or not appellee was the real party in interest as there was no evidence on the record of an assignment. Reversed for lack of standing.

.

Everhome Mortgage Company v. Rowland, No. 07AP-615 (Ohio 2008). Mortgagee was not the real party in interest pursuant to Rule 17(a). Lack of standing.

.

In **Lambert v. Firstar Bank, 83 Ark. App. 259, 127 S.W. 3d 523 (2003)**, complying with the Statutory Foreclosure Act does not insulate a financial institution from liability and does not prevent a party from timely asserting any claims or defenses it may have concerning a mortgage foreclosure A.C.A. §18-50-116(d)(2) and violates honest services Title 18 Fraud. Notice to credit reporting agencies of overdue payments/foreclosure on a fraudulent debt is defamation of character and a whole separate fraud.

A Court of Appeals does not consider assertions of error that are unsupported by convincing legal authority or argument, unless it is apparent without further research that the argument is well taken. FRAUD is a point well taken! Lambert Supra.

.

No lawful consideration tendered by Original Lender and/or Subsequent Mortgage and/or Servicing Company to support the alleged debt. "A lawful consideration must exist and be tendered to support the Note" and demand under TILA full disclosure of any such consideration. **Anheuser-Busch Brewing Company v. Emma Mason, 44 Minn. 318, 46 N.W. 558 (1890).**

.

National Banks and/or subsidiary Mortgage companies cannot retain the note, "Among the assets of the state bank were two notes, secured by mortgage, which could not be transferred to the new bank as assets under the National Banking Laws. **National Bank Act, Sect 28 & 56" National Bank of Commerce v. Atkinson, 8 Kan. App. 30, 54 P. 8 (1898).**

.

"A bank can lend its money, but not its credit." **First Nat'l Bank of Tallapoosa v. Monroe, 135 Ga 614, 69 S.E. 1123 (1911).**

.

It is not necessary for rescission of a contract that the party making the misrepresentation should have known that it was false, but recovery is allowed even though misrepresentation is innocently made, because it would be unjust to allow one who made false representations, even innocently, to retain the fruits of a bargain induced by such representations." Whipp v. Iverson, 43 Wis. 2d 166, 168 N.W.2d 201 (1969).

"A bank is not the holder in due course upon merely crediting the depositors account." **Bankers Trust v. Nagler, 23 A.D.2d 645, 257 N.Y.S.2d 298 (1965).**

.

"Any conduct capable of being turned into a statement of fact is representation. There is no distinction between misrepresentations effected by words and misrepresentations effected by other acts." (The seller or lender) "He is liable, not upon any idea of benefit to himself, but because of his wrongful act and the consequent injury to the other party." **Leonard v. Springer, 197 III 532. 64 NE 299 (1902).**

.

"If any part of the consideration for a promise be illegal, or if there are several considerations for an un-severable promise one of which is illegal, the promise, whether written or oral, is wholly void, as it is impossible to say what part or which one of the considerations induced the promise." **Menominee River Co. v. Augustus Spies L & C Co.,147 Wis. 559 at p. 572; 132 NW 1118 (1912).**

.

"The contract is void if it is only in part connected with the illegal transaction and the promise single or entire." **Guardian Agency v. Guardian Mut. Savings Bank, 227 Wis. 550, 279 NW 79 (1938).**

.

Moore v. Mid-Penn Consumer Discount Co., Civil Action No. 90-6452 U.S. Dist. LEXIS 10324 (Pa. 1991). The court held that, under TILA's Regulation Z, 12 CFR §226.4 (a), a lender had to expressly notify a borrower that he had a choice of insurer.

.

Marshall v. Security State Bank of Hamilton, 121 B.R. 814 (III. 1990) violation of Federal Truth in Lending 15 USCS §1638(a)(9), and Regulation Z. The bank took a security interest in the vehicle without disclosing the security interest.

.

Steinbrecher v. Mid-Penn Consumer Discount Co., 110 B.R. 155 (Pa. 1990). Mid-Penn violated TILA by not including in a finance charge the debtors' purchase of fire insurance on their home. The purchase of such insurance was a condition imposed by the company. The cost of the insurance was added to the amount financed and not to the finance charge.

.

Nichols v. Mid-Penn Consumer Discount Co., 1989 WL 46682 (Pa. 1989). Mid-Penn misinformed Nichols in the Notice of Right to Cancel Mortgage.

.

McElvany v. Household Finance Realty Corp., 98 B.R. 237 (Pa. 1989). debtor filed an application to remove the mortgage foreclosure proceedings to the United States District Court pursuant to 28 USCS §1409. It is strict liability in the sense that absolute compliance is required and even technical violations will form the basis for liability. Lauletta v. Valley Buick Inc., 421 F. Supp. 1036 at 1040 (Pa. 1976).

.

Johnson-Allen v. Lomas and Nettleton Co., 67 B.R. 968 (Pa. 1986). Violation of Truth-in-Lending Act requirements, 15 USCS §1638(a)(10), required mortgagee to provide a statement containing a description of any security interest held or to be retained or acquired. Failure to disclose.

.

Cervantes v. General Electric Mortgage Co., 67 B.R. 816 (Pa. 1986). creditor failed to meet disclosure requirements under the Truth in Lending Act, 15 U.S.C.S. § 1601-1667c and Regulation Z of the Federal Reserve Board, 12 CFR §226.1

McCausland v. GMAC Mortgage Co., 63 B.R. 665, (Pa. 1986). GMAC failed to provide information which must be disclosed as defined in the TILA and Regulation Z, 12 CFR §226.1

.

Perry v. Federal National Mortgage Corp., 59 B.R. 947 (Pa. 1986) the disclosure statement was deficient under the Truth In Lending Act, 15 U.S.C.S. § 1638(a)(9). Defendant Mortgage Co. failed to reveal clearly what security interest was retained.

.

Schultz v. Central Mortgage Co., 58 B.R. 945 (Pa. 1986). The court determined creditor mortgagor violated the Truth In Lending Act, 15 U.S.C.S. § 1638(a)(3), by its failure to include the cost of mortgage insurance in calculating the finance charge. The court found creditor failed to meet any of the conditions for excluding such costs and was liable for twice the amount of the true finance charge.

.

Solis v. Fidelity Consumer Discount Co., 58 B.R. 983 (Pa. 1986). Any misgivings creditors may have about the technical nature of the requirements should be addressed to Congress or the Federal Reserve Board, not the courts. Disclosure requirements for credit sales are governed by 15 U.S.C.S. § 1638 12 CFR § 226.8(b), (c). Disclosure requirements for consumer loans are governed by 15 U.S.C.S. § 1639 12 CFR § 226.8(b), (d). A violator of the disclosure requirements is held to a standard of strict liability. Therefore, a plaintiff need not show that the creditor in fact deceived him by making substandard disclosures. Since Transworld Systems Inc. have not cancelled the security interest and return all monies paid by Ms. Sherrie I. LaForce within the 20 days of receipt of the letter of rescission of October 7, 2009, the lenders named above are responsible for actual and statutory damages pursuant to 15 U.S.C. 1640(a).

.

Porter v. Mid-Penn Consumer Discount Co., 961 F.2d 1066 (3rd Cir. 1992). Porter filed an adversary proceeding against appellant under 15 U.S.C. §1635, for failure to honor her request to rescind a loan secured by a mortgage on her home.

.

Rowland v. Magna Millikin Bank of Decatur, N.A., 812 F.Supp. 875 (1992) Even technical violations will form the basis for liability. The mortgagors had a right to rescind the contract in accordance with 15 U.S.C. §1635(c).

.

New Maine Nat. Bank v. Gendron, 780 F.Supp. 52 (1992). The court held that defendants were entitled to rescind loan under strict liability terms of TILA because plaintiff violated TILA's provisions.

Dixon v. S & S Loan Service of Waycross, Inc., 754 F.Supp. 1567 (1990); TILA is a remedial statute, and, hence, is liberally construed in favor of borrowers. The remedial objectives of TILA are achieved by imposing a system of strict liability in favor of consumers when mandated disclosures have not been made. Thus, liability will flow from even minute deviations from the requirements of the statute and the regulations promulgated under it.

.

Woolfolk v. Van Ru Credit Corp., 783 F.Supp. 724 (1990) There was no dispute as to the material facts that established that the debt collector violated the FDCPA. The court granted the debtors' motion for summary judgment and held that (1) under 15 U.S.C. §1692(e), a debt collector could not use any false, deceptive, or misleading representation or means in connection with the collection of any debt; Unfair Debt Collection Practices Act.

.

Jenkins v. Landmark Mortg. Corp. of Virginia, 696 F.Supp. 1089 (W.D. Va. 1988). Plaintiff was also misinformed regarding the effects of a rescission. The pertinent regulation states that "when a consumer rescinds a transaction, the security interest giving rise to the right of rescission becomes void and the consumer shall not be liable for any amount, including any finance charge." 12 CFR §226.23(d) (1).

.

Laubach v. Fidelity Consumer Discount Co., 686 F.Supp. 504 (E.D. Pa. 1988). monetary damages for the plaintiffs pursuant to the Racketeer Influenced and Corrupt Organization Act, 18 USC §1961. (Count I); the Truth-in-Lending Act, 15 USC §1601.

.

Searles v. Clarion Mortg. Co., 1987 WL 61932 (E.D. Pa. 1987); Liability will flow from even minute deviations from requirements of the statute and Regulation Z. failure to accurately disclose the property in which a security interest was taken in connection with a consumer credit transaction involving the purchase of residential real estate in violation of 15 USCs §1638(a)(9). and 12 CFR §226.18(m).

.

Dixon v. S & S Loan Service of Waycross, Inc., 754 F.Supp. 1567, 1570 (S.D. Ga. 1990). Congress's purpose in passing the Truth in Lending Act (TILA), 15 USCs §1601(a). was to assure a meaningful disclosure of credit terms so that the consumer will be able to compare more readily the various credit terms available to him. 15 USCs §1601(a). TILA is a remedial statute, and, hence, is liberally construed in favor of borrowers.;

.

Cervantes v. General Electric Mortgage Co., 67 B.R. 816 (E.D. Pa. 1986). The court found that the TILA violations were governed by a strict liability standard, and defendant's failure to reveal in the disclosure statement the exact nature of the security interest violated the TILA.

.

Perry v. Federal National Mortgage, 59 B.R. 947 (E.D. Pa. 1986). Defendant failed to accurately disclose the security interest taken to secure the loan.

.

Porter v. Mid-Penn Consumer Discount Co., 961 F.2d 1066 (3rd Cir. 1992). Adversary proceeding against appellant under 15 U.S.C. §1635, for failure to honor her request to rescind a loan secured by a mortgage on her home. She was entitled to the equitable relief of rescission and the statutory remedies under 15 U.S.C. §1640 for appellant's failure to rescind upon request.

.

Solis v. Fidelity Consumer Discount Co., 58 B.R. 983 (Pa. 1986). Any misgivings creditors may have about the technical nature of the requirements should be addressed to Congress or the Federal Reserve Board, not the courts. Disclosure requirements for credit sales are governed by 15 U.S.C.S. § 1638 12 CFR § 226.8(b), (c). Disclosure requirements for consumer loans are governed by 15 U.S.C.S. § 1639 12 CFR § 226.8(b), (d).

.

A violator of the disclosure requirements is held to a standard of strict liability. Therefore, a plaintiff need not show that the creditor in fact deceived him by making substandard disclosures. Rowland v. Magna Millikin Bank of Decatur, N.A., 812 F.Supp. 875 (1992),

.

Even technical violations will form the basis for liability. The mortgagors had a right to rescind the contract in accordance with 15 U.S.C. §1635(c). New Maine Nat. Bank v. Gendron, 780 F.Supp. 52 (D. Me. 1992). The court held that defendants were entitled to rescind loan under strict liability terms of TILA because plaintiff violated TILA's provisions.

Google:

"The Boyko Decision"

"Rickie Walker Case"

There are so many others, we can publish a whole Bible sized handbook, but frankly, it's pretty boring...

RECOMMENDED PRODUCTS

JURISDICTIONARY

Can't afford a lawyer? Then this product is for you.

This is the complete Pro Se guide to litigation. If you want to go to court, you must absolutely understand the rules of court. Jurisdictionary offers you a quick introduction to help you understand the framework of court.

What is a Motion?

What is a proper Cause of Action to be considered Legally sufficient?

How do you make the Judge follow the law?

If you don't know the answers to these, how will you stand a chance in court?

Even if you hire a lawyer, how do you know they are doing a good job for you? How do you know what questions to ask your lawyer to make sure that he is representing you properly if you are ignorant? Your lawyer could be taking you to the cleaners.

If you plan to go to court, don't you dare go without Jurisdictionary.

For more information about Jurisdictionary, come to http://www.consumerdefenseprograms.com. Look under the Resources menu for Jurisdictionary.

AFFORDABLE MORTGAGE SCENE INVESTIGATION SECURITIZATION AUDITS

Having a MSI Securitization audit is like having a picture of your banker in the vault, stuffing money into his bag after hours (ie. Caught in the act of stealing). Bankers absolutely hate these as it exposes their fraud.

There are many so called "securitization auditors" out there who promise the world. Unless you actually know what to look for, you could be wasting your money. We've investigated quite a number of auditors, and many of them are scams or are simply way too expensive for the average homeowner. Some charge as much as $2000, while some attorneys charge as much as $4000 for an audit because they know the power an audit can have.

Before you can bring a civil action against your lender, you will need to have proof. Without sufficient proof, your case is subject to dismissal.

Having a MSI securitization audit will ensure that your case will be able to survive a Motion to Dismiss to get into the Discovery phase of the civil action.

To order a MSI securitization audit, come to:

http://www.consumerdefenseprograms.com/resources/securitization-audit/

BANKRUPTCY PREPARATION SERVICE

Preparing paperwork for a bankruptcy is very complicated and is not recommended that you do this on your own.

Our specialty Bankruptcy Preparation Service is designed for the homeowner in foreclosure in mind. Our Specialists have been helping foreclosure clients file bankruptcy paperwork for over 5 years.

For more information about our specialty Bankruptcy Preparation Service, come to:

http://www.consumerdefenseprograms.com/ resources/bankruptcy-preparation-services/

Made in the USA
Middletown, DE
18 February 2023

25172805R00096